HOW TO GROW ANNUALS & PERENNIALS

Expert advice on growing a host of varied plants, with a practical guide to gardening skills for all situations, climates and garden styles

HOW TO GROW ANNUALS & PERENNIALS

Expert advice on growing a host of varied plants, with a practical guide to gardening skills for all situations, climates and garden styles

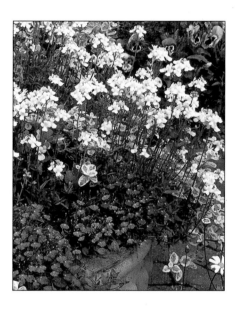

Step-by-step techniques and more than 270 stunning photographs

Richard Bird

southwater

Dedicated with love to Jenny Cline, for all her help and inspiration in the garden

This edition is published by Southwater

Southwater is an imprint of Anness Publishing Ltd
Hermes House, 88–89 Blackfriars Road, London SE1 8HA
tel. 020 7401 2077; fax 020 7633 9499
www.southwaterbooks.com; www.annesspublishing.com

If you like the images in this book and would like to investigate using them
for publishing, promotions or advertising, please visit our website
www.practicalpictures.com for more information.

© Anness Publishing Ltd 2006

UK agent: The Manning Partnership Ltd
6 The Old Dairy, Melcombe Road, Bath BA2 3LR
tel. 01225 478444; fax 01225 478440; sales@manning-partnership.co.uk

UK distributor: Grantham Book Services Ltd
Isaac Newton Way, Alma Park Industrial Estate, Grantham, Lincs NG31 9SD
tel. 01476 541080; fax 01476 541061; orders@gbs.tbs-ltd.co.uk

North American agent/distributor: National Book Network
4501 Forbes Boulevard, Suite 200, Lanham, MD 20706
tel. 301 459 3366; fax 301 429 5746; www.nbnbooks.com

Australian agent/distributor: Pan Macmillan Australia
Level 18, St Martins Tower, 31 Market St, Sydney, NSW 2000
tel. 1300 135 113; fax 1300 135 103; customer.service@macmillan.com.au

New Zealand agent/distributor: David Bateman Ltd
30 Tarndale Grove, Off Bush Road, Albany, Auckland
tel. (09) 415 7664; fax (09) 415 8892

Publisher: Joanna Lorenz
Editorial Director: Helen Sudell
Editors: Ann Kay and Elizabeth Woodland
Designer: Michael Morey
Cover Designer: Balley Design Associates
Production Controller: Steve Lang

Previously published as part of a larger volume, *A Gardener's Guide to Annuals and Perennials*

Main front cover image shows *Begonia semperflorens*

10 9 8 7 6 5 4 3 2 1

Note: Bracketed terms are intended for American readers

ACKNOWLEDGEMENTS
Unless listed below, photographs are © Anness Publishing Ltd
t=top; b=bottom; c=centre; r=right; l=left
RICHARD BIRD PLANT PICTURES: 43b; 46b; 76t; 84tl; 84tr. PETER MCHOY: 82b.
The publishers would also like to thank: Peter Anderson and Ray Cox for their work on
the photography and Unwins for giving access to their grounds for photography.

Contents

INTRODUCTION

In spite of a modern tendency for television personalities to create gardens with few or no plants, there is no doubt in most people's minds that without plants a garden is simply not a garden. There is something about the presence of plants – their colour, shape and fragrance – that lifts the spirits in a very special way. Annuals and perennials are the two most popular types of flowering plants, offering a vast selection of ways to add that vital colour and stimulus to every kind of garden.

Enjoying plants

Plants give pleasure to people in many different ways. The majority of gardeners enjoy filling space with colour, shape and texture as well as planning a garden to make the most of their chosen plants' strong points. There are others for whom it is the plant itself that is of principal interest. They are less interested in how the plant fits into the overall picture of the garden, or indeed how the garden

Anyone can produce this magnificent array of dahlias, verbenas and salvias. It remains colourful for a long period – from midsummer well into autumn.

looks as a whole, and are more absorbed by growing a particular type of plant to absolute perfection. These gardeners may only grow plants in order to show them, or simply because they enjoy the challenge of growing rare and difficult types.

There are others still who garden simply because they enjoy working in the open air and get a real joy from cultivation. For them it is the process as well as the results that matter. The huge variety of annuals and perennials that are available, and the many ways in which they can be grown, can easily cater to all these different approaches.

Starting out

Tackling a large bare patch may seem a rather daunting task to somebody who has not done any gardening before, but it is nothing like as difficult as some experts would have you believe.

Gardening is rather like decorating a room: naturally a certain amount of time and effort is involved, but if you are not satisfied with the result you can always change it. This is particularly true

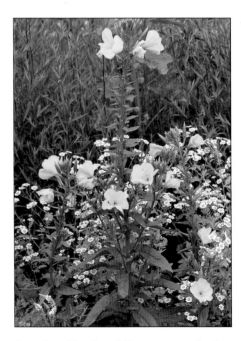

Oenothera biennis and *Tanacetum parthenium* produce a fine yellow and white scheme.

This border mixes annuals, hardy perennials and tender perennials treated as annuals.

This selection of perennials, growing beside water, shows the vast range of shapes and textures that can be used as well as the value of foliage.

right next year, or even the year after. Having said that, there are, of course, basic sensible and effective practices that have developed over many generations, and all of these are clearly outlined in this book.

Discovering plants

Plants form the basis of all good gardens. They are the key elements in any gardern design. Plants create not only form and structure, but can also provide wonderful scent and colour, and they also give a tremendous amount of joy and pleasure, both in their final appearance and in the satisfaction of growing them.

As you develop your garden you will become more interested in certain plants rather than others. You will then be able to create your own database of information from nursery catalogues, magazines, books and the internet. Soon you may even find that you have turned into one of those gardeners for whom studying plants is as fascinating as actually growing them.

with annual plants as they give you the opportunity to start from scratch each year.

Working with colour

Many beginners are worried about combining colours, but the key is simply to go for plants and effects that you like without worrying about what other people do.

Remember that we all have some ability where colour is concerned: we choose what goes with what when we get dressed each day and we choose colours for decorating and furnishing our homes. Planning a garden is really no different. In the same way that there are fashion magazines to help you choose your style, so there is no shortage of different kinds of gardening magazine to browse through for inspiration, and there is nothing more enjoyable than wandering around other people's gardens in search of good ideas.

Learning the ropes

There is also no need to worry about gardening techniques. Most gardening is common sense and if you do make a mistake, just remember that you can always put it

An informal container – featuring annual sweet peas, tender verbenas and perennial violas – demonstrates just how effectively annuals and perennials can be mixed.

Choosing plants for your garden

Selecting plants on aesthetic grounds alone – for form or flower colour, for instance – is not really a successful method of gardening, though nearly all gardeners fall victim to some ravishing specimen spotted at a garden centre or garden show. Since not all plants will thrive in the same conditions, it makes sense to limit your choice to what will do well in your garden. One of the most important lessons for any gardener is that you cannot grow what you want wherever you please.

The plants chosen for this scheme, including *Artemisia* and *Sisyrinchium*, are perfectly adapted to hot, dry conditions.

The aspect

Light is essential to all plants as it provides the energy that is needed to manufacture food during daylight hours, so providing the right levels of light is crucial if the plants are to thrive. For this reason, one of the first considerations is the aspect of your garden. You will need to study your garden to work out which areas are sunny, shady or in partial shade at different times of the day. In their natural environment, some plants will grow in dense shade on the forest floor while others are exposed to intense bright sunlight for long periods of time. This wide diversity of natural habitat explains why so many of the different ornamental plants we grow require different conditions. The ability to adapt to unfamiliar conditions is a major reason for the popularity of many common plants.

The soil

It is worth finding out whether your soil is acid or alkaline, since not all plants will do equally well in both (though the majority are indifferent). The most reliable method is with a chemical soil testing kit, or you can make an educated guess by looking to see what is growing successfully in the surrounding countryside, or in other people's gardens if you live in a built-up area. Geological maps also indicate the presence of limestone or silt, for instance.

Equally important, perhaps more so, is the soil profile. The ideal – a loam that binds easily into crumbs, allowing for both moisture-retention and free drainage of excess water – suits nearly all plants. Stiff clays, cold and heavy to work, are usually nutrient high, suiting bog plants and others adapted to reliably wet conditions. Dry, sandy soils, easy to work and quick to warm up in spring, are nutrient poor but are the ideal medium for many of the Mediterranean plants and herbs. All soils can be improved by digging in

Dainty *Iris sibirica* is one of the many irises that appreciate a damp site. It looks exquisite grown near to water.

organic matter, in the form of garden compost or well-rotted farmyard manure, greatly increasing the range of plants you can grow.

If a plant is doing well in your garden, either plant more of the same, or some of its near relatives or others that enjoy the same conditions. The reverse is also true. If you have trouble establishing a particular plant, you are also unlikely to succeed with others of its ilk.

Designing with plants

A garden is more than just a collection of plants, and relies for much of its impact on the way these are grouped together. If you have a flair for design, devising effective groupings may be no problem. If you do not, there are any number of strategies you can adopt that will lead to pleasing combinations.

When choosing plants for beds and borders, formal gardens for instance tend to dictate themselves. A formal rose garden will clearly feature roses, with only the "filler" plants left debatable. An island bed is meant to be viewed from all sides, so the tallest plants will usually go in the centre and smaller ones around the edges. Try planting a small tree such as *Malus floribunda* to create plenty of height.

Most gardens will feature single-sided borders, and the secret of a successful design is planning for a long period of interest. A border will not remain attractive for more than a month if all the plants flower briefly, at the same time. The plants you choose should also not only look pleasing when flowering, but also when out of bloom. A series of plants that bloom at different times can lead to an uncoordinated appearance of plants in flower dotted amid swathes of foliage at varying stages of growth. If you have space you can easily devote separate borders for spring, summer and autumn/winter interest. Otherwise, try a mixed border incorporating many different kinds of plants arranged in bold groups, rather than as isolated specimens. If you want to cut down on the regular replanting work, you can also use dwarf shrubs as backbone plants, then include flowering ground-cover plants, such as hardy geraniums and spring bulbs, to provide flowers over a long period.

The following pages should help you make the most out of annuals and perennials in your garden.

Here, tulips and primulas provide the interest before the standard roses come into bloom.

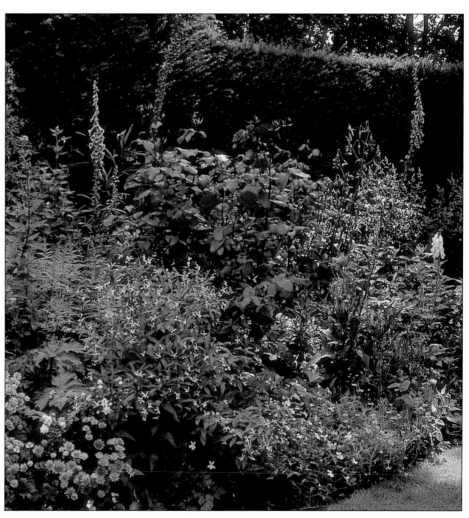

A classic mixed border, combining roses, lilies, and a range of easily pleased perennials against a backdrop of clipped yew.

Styling with annuals and perennials

Theoretically, there is no need to differentiate between annuals and perennials as they are both flowering or foliage plants. However, gardeners do tend to use them in slightly different ways. This is partly because of the annual's brief life and partly because annuals tend to be more brightly coloured than perennials, lending themselves to vivid displays. Perennials are more permanent and, although some do have bright colours, they are usually more muted.

In this section we look at the differing roles that the two types of plants can play. We also look at the different ways in which they can be combined to create a range of gardening styles, varying from the informality of the traditional cottage garden to the more clinical lines of a formal garden, where symmetry is all.

Generally, the style of a garden reflects its owner's lifestyle and personality. Gardens should always have a positive and uplifting atmosphere, so there is no point in creating a place where you feel uncomfortable. Use the following advice as guidance, but never be afraid to follow your own instinct.

A lovely cottage garden effect is created along this informal path using both annuals and perennials. The lush foliage helps to provide bulk.

Annuals and their role

Annuals are ephemeral plants: they flower for one season only and then they are gone. This may seem to be a disadvantage in a garden context, but in fact it can be a great benefit, especially for those gardeners who like to have something different in their beds each year.

What is an annual?

There are basically four different types of plant that are considered annuals from the garden point of view. The most common are the true annuals, which grow from seed, flower and produce their own seed within a year. There are many examples of these, but poppies and nasturtiums are popular ones. Closely allied to these are the biennials. These grow from seed one year and then flower during the next. Foxgloves and evening primroses are familiar examples.

Then there are those perennials that are tender, and so are treated as annuals and started afresh each year. Pelargoniums and busy Lizzies are good examples. Finally, there is another group of perennials that are used as annuals. These are simply

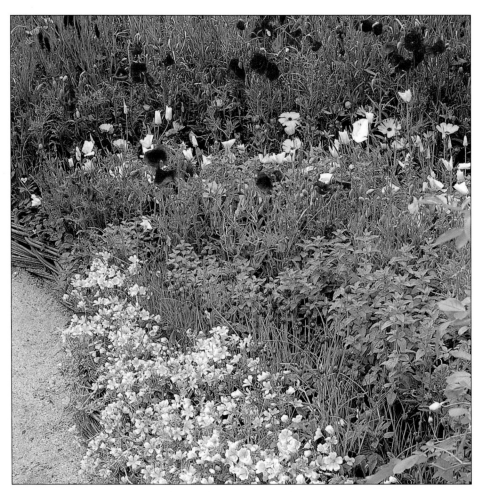

Limnanthes douglasii, the poached egg plant, creates a perfect border to this wildflower garden, which is dominated by annuals.

Hardiness

Since most annuals grow and flower within the year, hardiness may not seem to be an important factor to take into consideration, but it can be if you plan to grow your own annuals from seed. Hardy annuals can be sown outside and will withstand late frosts, but half-hardy or tender annuals must be raised under glass and not planted out until after the risk of frost has passed. Alternatively, half-hardy or tender annuals can be sown directly where they are to flower, but again only after the threat of frost is over.

short-lived perennials that are better grown from scratch each year. Frequently planted examples of these are wallflowers and sweet Williams.

Great diversity

One of the great advantages of using annuals is that the design of a garden need not be fixed: you can change the colour, texture and shape of the plantings each year if you wish. At the end of the flowering season you simply rip out the plants, then decide which annuals you want to plant for the next season. They come in all shapes, sizes and colours, so the gardener has a virtually limitless palette from which to create planting schemes. This versatility means that annuals can be used as massed bedding or mixed with other

plants, such as perennials, or they can be used in containers such as hanging baskets, large pots or window boxes. They also provide a wide range of flowers that can be cut for the house.

Annuals can be ideal for the smallest of spaces. Here, bright red pelargoniums are used very effectively in simple pots on a wall.

Long-flowering annuals

Ageratum
Antirrhinum majus
Argyranthemum
Begonia x semperflorens
Brachycome iberidifolia
Calendula officinalis
Impatiens
Lobelia erinus
Nicotiana
Pelargonium
Petunia
Salvia
Tagetes
Tropaeolum majus
Verbena x hybrida
Viola x wittrockiana
Zinnia elegans

Using annual plants is not all about making the most of showcasing the flowers. In this container, for example, silver foliage has been used to great effect.

Mixing it

Annuals can be used to great advantage mixed with perennials and shrubs. One big advantage that annuals have over perennials is that they tend to flower over long periods, often throughout the whole summer. So, in a mixed border, annuals can provide a permanent thread of colour.

Their temporary nature can also be put to good use. Often it will take several years before shrubs or perennials reach their final spread, and during this time there will be areas of bare earth around these plants. Annuals can readily be used here as attractive temporary fillers until the other plants eventually use up all of the space.

Annuals can also add a touch of lightness and almost frivolity to an otherwise staid border. For example, a border predominantly full of shrubs, perhaps planted for their interesting leaves, can be enlivened by massed plantings of bold summer annuals in front of and in between the shrubs. Each type of plant will complement the other.

Hanging displays

Annuals make wonderful container plants, whether in tubs, window boxes or hanging baskets. They usually last the whole season, providing constant attractive colour, though regular watering is a must for continuous flowering. Once the season is over, you can completely change your scheme for the following year simply by changing the plants. You might perhaps try hot oranges and reds one year, followed by softer, cooler blues and whites the next.

Pathways can provide a wonderful opportunity to display annuals to their full advantage. Change the colour and pattern each year to create a slightly different mood as you approach your front door.

Planning a bedding scheme and then watching it come to life can be a great deal of fun. Although not as popular currently as they once were, these schemes provide a stimulating challenge for the inventive mind.

Perennials and their role

When a dream garden springs into our minds, the linchpins of the borders will usually be the perennials, with their great wealth of colours, textures and forms. They provide an enormous selection of plants that will fit in with any style of gardening and will satisfy both the keen and lazy gardener.

What is a perennial?

Perennials are just what they say – perennial – though the description must be modified slightly, as it could apply to any plant that lasts more than a year. In fact, it generally applies to herbaceous material that is grown in general borders. In other words, it excludes trees, shrubs and plants that are grown in rock gardens or in greenhouses, even though these all might be long-lived. Most perennials die back in winter and then regenerate the following year, though some remain green right through the winter. From the gardening point of view, perennials are generally considered hardy – that is, they are able to withstand at least a certain amount of frost.

Changing scene

Most perennials have a relatively short flowering season. This may be seen as a disadvantage, but in fact it can be a great asset because it means that the garden is never static, it never becomes boring. It allows the borders to be planned in such a way that they present an ever-changing scene. It is possible, for example, to have a spring border of blue and yellow that transforms itself over the months into a pink and mauve border in the summer and then perhaps to hot colours for the autumn. Such coordination needs careful planning, of course, but that is half the fun of gardening.

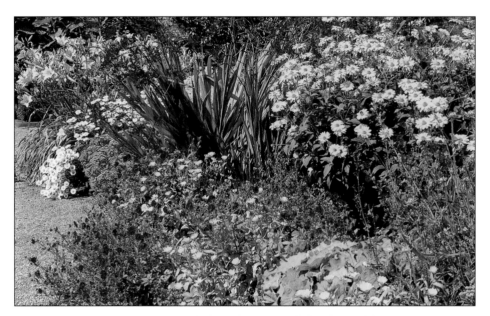

Use vivid, exciting colours to create a "hot" border. Just like beds of annual plants, herbaceous borders of perennials can be colour themed in all kinds of creative ways.

Foliage effect

Perennials are not only about flower colour. Many have interesting foliage in a wide range of colours, from greens, silvers and purples to yellows and creams. All these help to create a backdrop against which the flowers can be seen to advantage. Longer lasting than flowers, foliage forms the main structure of the borders throughout the growing season.

Herbaceous borders

Perennials can be used in many ways. One of the most effective is creating a herbaceous border entirely from perennials. These are usually planted in drifts, creating a sumptuous tapestry of colours through summer and autumn. Traditionally, herbaceous borders were found in large gardens, but smaller versions can easily be created to great effect.

This mixed border of perennials, annuals and shrubs shows the effects that can be achieved by combining a variety of different shapes, colours and textures.

Mixed borders

Many gardeners prefer to use a mixture of plants, perhaps using shrubs as the backbone and main structure of the garden and mixing in other plants to give differing colours throughout the year. Perennials are perfect for this role, particularly as there are a large number that like to grow in the light shade that is provided by being planted under or close to shrubs. Although shrubs form the structure, the perennials usually provide the majority of the plants. In some cases these may be a single large clump, but drifts of the bigger plants and carpets of the lower growing ones look better than scattering the plants around at random.

Potted perennials

It is often thought that the only place for perennials is in a large garden, but perennials are suited to all sizes of garden. They can be grown in a patio garden or even on a balcony or roof garden. As long as you are prepared to water them, they may be grown in containers, which can then be placed anywhere, including in gardens that are paved over and have no native soil at all.

Hardy perennials

Hardy perennials, as their name implies, are those that will tolerate frost and will reappear every year. Some tender perennials may be killed by frosts, although sometimes the frost will just kill off the exposed foliage, and the plant will regenerate from the roots. Although it is mainly temperature related, hardiness can be affected by soil conditions, and often a borderline plant will be more hardy in a free-draining soil than in a heavy damp one.

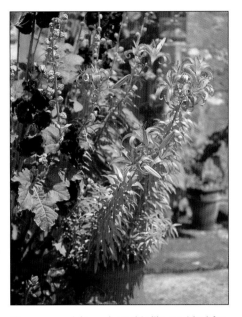

Many perennials, such as this lily, are ideal for tubs. Just move into position when in flower.

Plant-lovers

There are more varieties of perennial plants than any other type of plant available to the gardener. Some gardeners make a virtue of this and indulge their love of plants by creating special collections. Others collect a particular species, pinks (*Dianthus*) or hostas, for example, or favour broader groups – variegated plants are a very popular subject. There are also gardeners who seek out rare and difficult-to-grow plants, just to test their skills, and others who might make a collection of plants mentioned in, for example, the works of Shakespeare. The possibilities are almost endless.

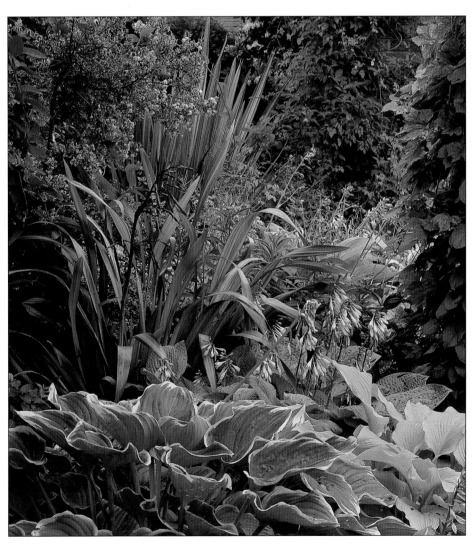

Perennials are not dependent on their flowers for their attraction. Many earn their keep as foliage plants, with the shapes and colour providing plenty of interest, as seen here.

Different styles of flower garden

There are various styles of garden to choose from, although there are no definitive rules and there is no reason why gardeners should not choose a mixture of designs. Having said that, there are a number of styles that have a proven track record, and it is perhaps worthwhile considering the pursuit of just one of them until you are confident enough to mix different styles.

In this cottage garden, the planting has seemingly been done at random and a wonderful mix of different types of plants creates a lively, natural atmosphere.

Lifestyle considerations

The basic advice is simple: choose a style of garden that you like. There are, however, various other factors that may be worth taking into consideration. Your lifestyle is one of the most important of these. However much you may like formal gardens, there is no point in designing a neat garden that needs to be kept in pristine condition in order to look its best if you are not naturally a tidy person or never have the time to keep it neat.

Likewise, a precise garden will be an uphill struggle if you have young children playing football or riding bicycles around and over the borders.

The family dog is also likely to have a say in this matter. A more informal style, which would be in keeping with your life, would be a more sensible and realistic choice. At a later stage in your life, a family garden may no longer be required, at which point, with possibly considerably more time on your hands, you could perhaps reconsider and think of other options.

Looking at the options

If you are new to gardening, you may have a vague idea of what you want but no firm idea about the reality. In this case, it will pay to spend a summer wandering around other gardens. Try to look at the best. The big gardens that are open to the public will have teams of gardeners at their beck and call, but there are still lessons and ideas to be learnt from them. A bit more realistic are the private gardens that open just once or twice a year. Most of these are designed and tended by their owners with little or no help. Look, make notes and, if you get the chance, talk to the owner and find out the problems and benefits of such a garden.

Another simple idea is to peer over fences (without being a nuisance) as you walk the dog and make critical appraisals of neighbouring gardens. What is right and what is wrong with them? What would you do to improve them? You can also watch television for inspiration, and look through gardening magazines and books.

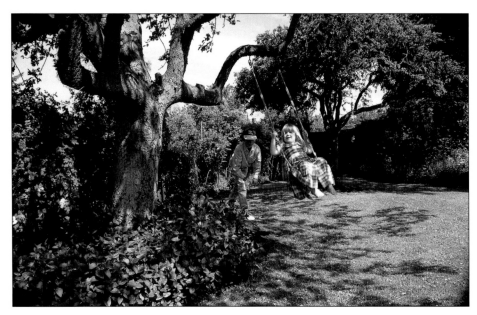

A family garden needs to take into account the interests and activities of all family members (including pets) and the gardener may have to make certain compromises.

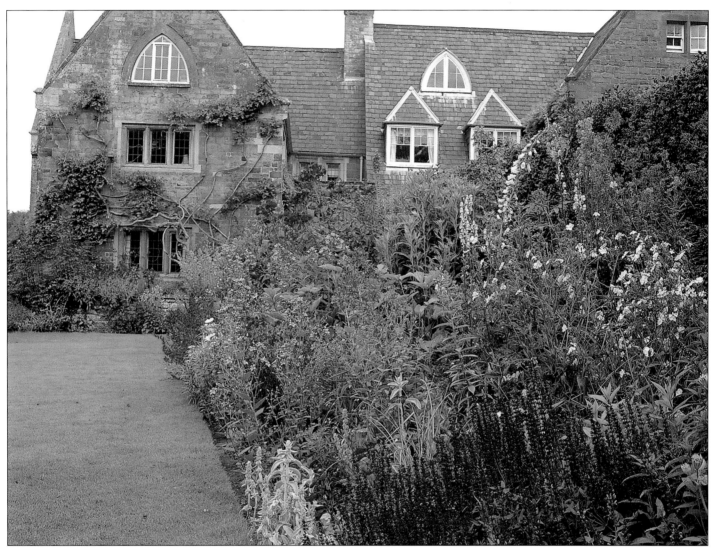

This predominantly herbaceous border also features a few roses. A keen gardener who loves to design with colour has been at work here.

Making notes

Some gardeners are able to keep detailed notes of what they see and ideas that they may adopt. Others are hopeless at this, and while they start out with good intentions, they soon run out of steam. One way around this is to take photographs as reminders. Another effective and low-effort method is to tear out pages from magazines that inspire you or leave markers tucked into books. Books and magazines can provide a really broad wealth of information, especially during the winter months when there is relatively little to look at in the gardens themselves.

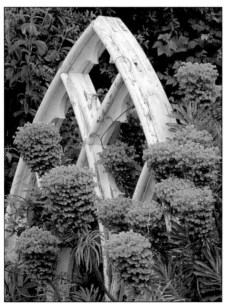

Look for simple but effective ideas such as this creative use of an old window frame.

Keep it simple

One of the biggest problems that new gardeners have is that they get carried away with their plans. They have grand ideas and can visualize just how their dream garden will look when finished, but they fail to consider the reality of the situation and to ask themselves some key questions. Is the garden big enough for all these ideas? Have they got enough money to pay for all the plants or hard landscaping that is required? And, above all, will they have the time not only to do the original work but also to maintain the garden once the initial enthusiasm has worn off?

Cottage gardens

Many people dream of a cottage in the country, with roses growing around the door and a feast of colour in the garden in front. Well, the good news is that you don't need to move to the country or even have a cottage to create such an attractive garden.

What is a cottage garden?

It is very difficult to define a cottage garden. We all know one when we see one, but describing them is not the easiest thing to do. Generally, they have an old-fashioned look. The real skill in creating a successful cottage garden is to design the borders to look as if they have not been designed at all. There is not much in the way of hard landscaping, just flowerbeds, and these are full to the brim with colourful plants.

Traditionally, the plants would be tough, hardy ones that needed little care. Most would be plants that had been grown for generations, such as primulas, hollyhocks, foxgloves and aquilegias. Today many new hybrids are considered suitable, especially if they are bright and brash.

Even containers can be given a cottage garden feel, simply by keeping them informal.

Cottage plants

Plants for a cottage garden tend, as has already been noted, to be old-fashioned plants that have been around for years. Many are annuals and biennials that self-sow, so the gardener does not have to think about new plants: they just appear.

One reason for using these old favourites, apart from their appearance, is that they are usually less prone to pests and diseases and hardier than many modern cultivars (which is why they have been around for a long time). In other words, they need little looking after. Unfortunately, some of these traditional plants, such as lupins and

Plants for a cottage garden

Alcea rosea
Anemone x hybrida
Aquilegia vulgaris
Aster novae-angliae
Aster novi-belgii
Astrantia major
Bellis perennis
Campanula portenschlagiana
Campanula persicifolia
Chrysanthemum
Dianthus (pinks)
Dicentra spectabilis
Doronicum
Geranium ibericum
Geum rivale
Lathyrus odoratus
Lilium candidum
Lupinus
Lysimachia nummularia
Meconopsis cambrica
Myrrhis odorata
Paeonia officinalis
Polemonium caeruleum
Primula
Pulmonaria
Saponaria officinalis
Sedum spectabile
Sempervivum
Stachys byzantina
Viola

Old-fashioned plants such as these polyanthus, forget-me-nots and aquilegias are perfect for spring in the cottage garden.

Some old-fashioned annuals, such as this *Collomia grandiflora* (the white flowers), have almost disappeared but are well worth searching out.

hollyhocks, have now developed diseases and pests, which makes them less reliable than they once were, though they can still be grown to great effect as short-lived plants.

The layout

If there is any characteristic to a cottage garden it is the hazy effect that all the intermingled colours create. The traditional image is one of a garden in which the plants seem to have been planted at random without any thought of planning. Gaps would be filled as they became available, and self-sowing plants would dot themselves around at will. Whether cottage gardens of the past really were this accidental or were just designed to look so, we may never actually know, but these days there is a tendency to exert at least a little control over the design in order to create the most pleasing picture that you can.

Getting it right

The backdrop to a cottage-garden style is important. For example, it will look better against an older

A path leading up to a cottage's front door is definitely at its most welcoming when it is lined with an abundance of interesting colours.

house than a modern one. This certainly doesn't mean that you have to live in a cottage in order to have a cottage garden. It just means that you must modify the situation somehow: for example, perhaps soften a modern house with roses, or create a cottage garden in the rear garden away from the house, dividing it off by using shrubs or trellising covered with climbers.

Although often claimed to be low-maintenance, cottage gardens do need a great deal of work. In summer, plenty of deadheading and tidying is required to prevent the garden looking a mess. Tight planting helps to reduce the amount of weeding and staking that is needed, but this can make access difficult when deadheading plants towards the back of the border.

A selection of vegetables

Most cottage gardens had a vegetable garden that had to supply produce for the family all year round. This often ran straight into the flower garden, with flowers and vegetables mixing where they met. Many vegetables have ornamental qualities and can happily be grown among flowers. A wigwam of runner beans, for example, is wonderful visually. Many vegetable gardens were also arranged in a decorative manner known as the potager. One big disadvantage of growing vegetables among the flowers or in a decorative manner is that gaps are left when you pick the produce.

This wonderful haze of colour typifies a cottage garden. It may look totally random and unplanned but a certain degree of clever control has been exercised.

Formal gardens

Gardens usually reflect their owners in one way or another. An untidy, relaxed person will often have an untidy and relaxed garden, whereas an elegant person who likes everything to be in its place may well opt for a formal garden. Such a garden is usually a positive feature of the home rather than just an outdoor space.

What is a formal garden?

Generally, a formal garden is one that has some formal qualities about it. This usually means that the shapes within the garden are geometric. Thus lines tend to be straight or in precise curves, such as a circle, rather than sinuous and informal. Beds are frequently square, rectangular or circular. Sometimes they might even be triangular, but this is an awkward shape in the garden because the corners are difficult to plant as well as being tricky to mow around.

Another aspect of formality is that there is often regular repetition, in other words certain plants or even whole beds may be repeated at regular intervals. This creates symmetry, which is an important part of such gardens. Calmness and tranquillity are the qualities that usually sum up the formal garden.

Sparseness

Formal gardens can contain as much planting as you like, but many rely on relatively few plants set in key positions. Often a round pond set in a gravelled area with just a couple of clumps of marginal plants – irises, perhaps, and a few water lilies – can look quite stunning in its simplicity. Long vistas down paths also create a feeling of calmness.

Formal plants

Any plants may be used in formal gardens, but there are many that are preferred because they have a formality about them either in their natural overall shape or the quality of the leaves. Others, mainly shrubs but also some ground-cover plants, lend themselves to being trimmed into formal shapes. Clumps of hostas and irises are valuable because of their regular leaf shapes, while grasses such as miscanthus or plants such as yucca or cordyline all have their fountains of leaves. Many ferns also produce this graceful fountain shape. Other plants that work very well in formal gardens are the

Straight lines and geometric patterns make this garden look very formal. Even the container has a symmetrical appearance.

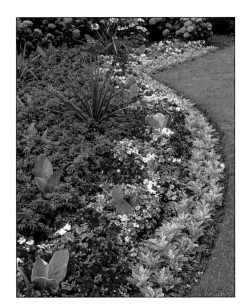

Bedding laid out in lines with a regular repeat of certain plants or colours is one way to add formality to a bed or a whole garden.

statuesque ones, such as verbascum. Annuals all of the same height, such as salvias, or in rounded clumps, such as busy Lizzies in a large container, can also contribute to a very formal look.

The role of containers

Containers can often play an extremely important part in a formal garden scheme, especially large ones filled with a single plant. A classic example is agapanthus placed at the

Plants for a formal garden

Good leaves or shape	
Agapanthus	Veratrum
Asplenium	Verbascum
Athyrium	Yucca
Bergenia	Zantedeschia
Cardiocrinum	
Cortaderia	**Good in-fill plants**
Crambe	Ageratum
Dierama	Alchemilla
Digitalis	Antirrhinum
Euphorbia	Bellis perennis
Foeniculum	Callistephus
Hosta	chinensis
Lilium	Diascia
Matteuccia	Lobelia erinus
struthiopteris	Myosotis sylvatica
Miscanthus	Nicotiana alata
Pennisetum	(N. affinis)
Sisyrinchium	Petunia
Stipa	Tagetes erecta
	Tagetes patula

entrance to a patio or at the bottom of some steps. Again, plants with a fountain shape, such as yucca or grasses, are ideal subjects for positions such as these. A series of pots set at regular intervals down a path is also a useful device. The pots can contain perennials, annuals or shrubs, but they should have a neat overall appearance.

Sculpture and dramatic containers, even if they do not contain plants, help to give the garden an air of formality.

Maintenance

Compared with many other types of garden, formal gardens are relatively easy to maintain, although at times it is more like housework than gardening. The general design rarely needs changing, so there is little planting unless you are using areas of bedding plants. With good mulching there should be little weeding, so it is mainly down to trimming and keeping the hard surfaces in good order.

Boxed in

Many formal gardens use box hedges to line paths or even to surround beds completely. In really extravagant gardens a series of box hedges are used to create a knot garden. The beds within these hedges may be restricted to one or two plant types, with annual bedding plants often used to paint blocks of colour within the green outlines of the box. This type of formal garden is often constructed on a grand scale, but it can be successfully emulated in smaller gardens.

Straight lines – whether they consist of low hedging or bedding plants (the latter is seen here) – and geometric shapes can create great clarity of design in a formal scheme.

Informal gardens

Most of us do not have the time to commit ourselves regularly to our garden, however much we wish we could. We also have conflicting demands on the garden: it is not just something beautiful or something to contemplate but also a place to live in and enjoy. So we end up creating an informal garden that suits our lifestyle. It is none the worse for that.

What is an informal garden?

An informal garden is everything a formal garden isn't. It is a garden designed around our tastes and lifestyle. The borders are full of plants that we like but not necessarily planted with military precision. The lines are not regular but comfortable and enjoyable, a bit like a favourite chair. There are lots of different things to see, but they are not necessarily connected in such a rigid way as in a formal garden. There is plenty of room for children to play, and no one gets too hysterical if a ball gets into the beds or the shape of a shrub is spoilt by being turned into a camp. The gardener still takes a lot of trouble over how it is planted and how it looks, but the garden carries with it an air of comfortable informality.

This spot in the garden is a wonderful place to relax, as it is surrounded by a comfortable, unstructured mixture of different types of plants.

Informal plants

Virtually any plant is suitable for an informal garden – that is the joy of this garden type (this is why no box containing a listing of recommended plants has been given here). It is the way in which plants are used, not the plants themselves, that is key.

What you could do if you wish is to create different areas for different plants. For example, if you are particularly fond of plants that favour damp conditions, you could make one area into a bog garden. Similarly, a rock garden or a gravel bed could be introduced for plants that tend to favour drier conditions. You can also create a more mixed garden, with annuals, perennials, climbers, shrubs and even trees, combined and arranged as you please. You could also experiment with using colours and textures in various creative ways.

There is certainly no formality here, and the gardener is free to remove or add plants without upsetting the balance of the scheme.

Here, the delightful edging to the path has all the colour but none of the rigid formality of a bedding scheme.

The importance of grass

Grass and hard surfaces have an important role to play in informal gardens. In many cases, such a garden will be a family one and grass has the obvious importance as a play area. But grass and surfaces also have a visual importance. If the whole garden is filled with flowering plants, the eye becomes restless: there is too much to see. An expanse of grass gives the eye a chance to rest and acts as a foil to the liveliness of the borders.

The edge of the grass, paving or path also acts as a defining limit to the border by creating an edge, which, again, is very important visually. Such an area of grass does not have to be kept pristine, mown with perfect stripes. It can be a hard-wearing, everyday sort of lawn, which copes with bicycles and ball games, and still has just the same visual effect.

Maintenance

Informal gardens can become rather high in maintenance, particularly if irregular attention is given to them. It is an inescapable fact that garden jobs don't just go away if they are ignored, they just get bigger. So if you leave the weeding for a few weeks, the effort to rid the borders of weeds can become a daunting task that takes a long time to do. Similarly, if herbaceous perennials and shrubs are left growing, with no attention paid to them, they will merrily go on growing until the garden becomes almost over-run and a major operation is needed to get everything back to the original plan. It is therefore important to do a little bit of work often rather than a lot in sudden bursts. With a little bit of attention, informal gardens are easy to maintain.

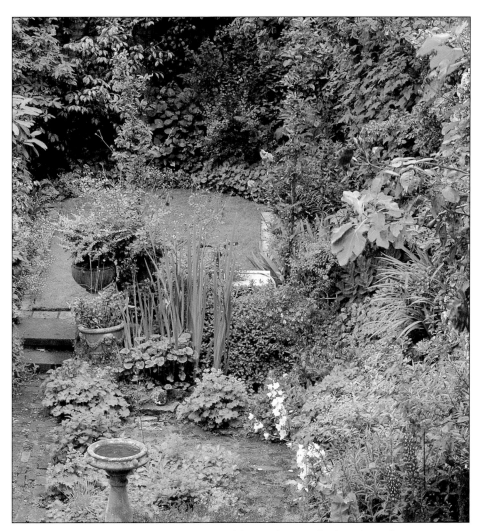

The seemingly random but not untidy nature of this garden is really charming. It has a delightfully informal, but still cared for, appearance.

Containers can be used just as much in informal arrangements as they are in formal gardens. They are especially useful for providing temporary fills.

Wildflower gardens

With the increasing reduction of wild habits for many plants, many people have begun to look afresh at what they are losing and have gained an appreciation of their native flora. This has encouraged them to create areas within their own garden in which wild flowers can flourish, partly to help to preserve these flowers and partly because they simply enjoy them.

What is a wildflower garden?

A wildflower garden is one in which native flowers are grown in as near wild conditions as possible. The idea of wild conditions is not so much to create a picturesque landscape but more to create conditions in which the flowers will grow.

There are several types of garden all based on habitats in the wild. The most common is a wildflower meadow. Next are those based on plants of the cornfield and arable land, which like the disturbed soil of the open border. Then there are the woodland plants that need a shady garden. Finally, there are the wetland plants, which need a pond, stream or boggy area. Once established, wildflower gardens or borders are

The pretty *Anemone nemorosa* is an easy, non-invasive plant to grow. Plant it under shrubs or under a hedgerow.

wonderful for attracting native birds and insects. They are, after all, their natural food.

When planning a wildflower garden, do not source your plants from those growing in the wild. Although they seem to be there for the gathering, always resist the temptation and buy seed from a respectable seed merchant instead. Leave the plants in the wild for others to enjoy.

Wildflower meadows

These are best created by first sowing grass or using an existing lawn. Once the "meadow" has become established, mow it regularly to eliminate the coarser grasses. Now is the time to plant the wildflowers. They are more likely to become established if you grow the plants from seed in pots and then transplant them into the grass than if you simply scatter the seed. Prevent rank grass from taking over by mowing in high summer after the plants have seeded and then at least a couple more times before winter sets in. Do not leave the grass lying after cutting.

Cornfield plants

Many wildflowers will not grow in grass, needing disturbed soil to flourish. Poppies, cornflowers and corn marigolds are examples of these. They are mainly annuals and can be grown from seed in pots and then transplanted or sown directly from seed. Once established, they will self-sow and then reappear every year. A border can be devoted to them or they can be mixed into a general border.

Here it is early spring in the meadow garden, with *Fritilaria meleagris*, the snake's head fritillary, making a welcome appearance.

Non-invasive grasses are ideal for wildflower gardens. This is the annual *Hordeum jubatum*, sparkling in the sun.

Chrysanthemum segetum is one of many cornfield flowers that are ideal for wildflower beds.

in deciduous woods and put in an appearance in the early spring before the trees come into leaf. This is so that they get enough sun and rain to grow and develop. Primroses, wood anemones and bluebells are good examples of these. It is not necessary to have a wood in order to grow them – they will be quite happy growing under deciduous shrubs and a good use of space.

Water plants

These can be a bit more problematic in that many native water or bog plants can be rather rampant and tend to take over. They need good management to keep them under control. The conditions that these plants enjoy are also very conducive to weeds, so be prepared for regular weeding. They can be grown in the same way as any other water- or bog-loving plants.

Woodland plants

There are a number of woodland species that make very attractive planting in shady areas, perhaps under shrubs or trees or perhaps on the sunless side of a house or fence. Most woodland flowers tend to grow

Plants for a wildflower garden

Wildflower meadows
Achillea millefolium
Campanula rotundifolia
Cardamine pratensis
Centaurea scabiosa
Geranium pratense
Hypericum perforatum
Leontodon hispidus
Malva moschata
Narcissus pseudonarcissus
Primula veris
Ranunculus acris
Succisa pratensis

Cornfield plants
Centaurea cyanus
Chrysanthemum segetum
Papaver rhoeas

Woodland plants
Anemone nemorosa
Convallaria majalis
Digitalis purpurea
Hyacinthoides non-scripta
Primula vulgaris

Water gardens
Butomus umbellatus
Caltha palustris
Eupatorium cannabinum
Filipendula ulmaria
Iris pseudacorus
Mentha aquatica

Although normally considered a border plant, *Camassia* makes an excellent plant for the wild meadow garden.

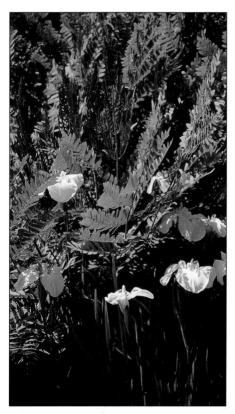

Ferns make good plants for shady areas of wildflower gardens. In wetter areas the royal fern, *Osmunda regalis*, is ideal.

Coping with different conditions

Sometimes we are lucky enough when buying a house to get one with a garden that offers us pretty much what we wanted, or at least offering excellent growing conditions. If we are very lucky, we may even be able to choose the house specifically for the garden. However, for most of us, we select the house and then simply have to accept the garden along with it. This can present the keen gardener with a variety of situations, both in terms of weather and soil conditions. Although the weather cannot be altered, quite a bit can be done to improve the soil and make it suitable for our chosen plants. Alternatively, we can just decide to accept what the garden offers, and select those plants that like a wide range of conditions. Similarly, the size of the garden is usually predetermined, with little chance of increasing it. Again, it is perfectly possible to create a delightful garden within the constraints that this puts upon you.

Over the next few pages we look at the most important conditions under which you may have to create a garden. Very few gardeners start from scratch, as there is usually some form of garden already in existence, giving some indication of the conditions you might expect there.

Making the most of the slope, this gravel garden is ideal for growing dry-loving and sun-loving plants.

Dry gardens

Once upon a time there was only one type of dry garden – one that was naturally so. Nowadays, with the increasing desire to create a number of habitats in which to grow the widest range of plants, many gardeners set out actually to create these conditions. In either case, there are a large number of varied annuals and perennials that suit a dry environment.

Dry conditions

Just because a garden is dry does not necessarily mean that it receives very little rain. There are many gardens that receive a lot of rain and yet are still dry under foot. The reason for this is that the soil is very free-draining and any moisture that falls, either from clouds or from a watering can, passes quickly through it. These are mainly sandy or gravelly soil, but chalky soils can also be very free-draining. As well as losing water quickly, many dry soils are also poor in terms of nutrients. The water passing through leeches out the nutrients, taking the food that plants require well below the level of their roots. Many seaside gardens are of this nature.

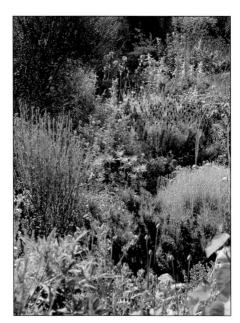

A surprisingly large number of plants like dry conditions and a very attractive garden can be built around them.

Plants for dry gardens

Allium	Glaucium flavum
hollandicum	Lavatera
Argemone	Onopordon
Artemisia	acanthium
Atriplex hortensis	Ophiopogon
Bergenia	planiscapus
Canna	'Nigrescens'
Centranthus	Papaver
Cerinthe major	somniferum
Cortaderia	Pennisetum
Crambe	Salvia
Elymus	Sedum
Eryngium	Stachys
Eschscholzia	byzantinus
Euphorbia	Verbascum
Foeniculum	Yucca

Altering the conditions

It is possible to increase the water-retentiveness of dry soil so that you can grow a much wider range of plants in it. This is done by adding well-rotted organic material to the soil when you dig it. Garden compost (soil mix) or farmyard

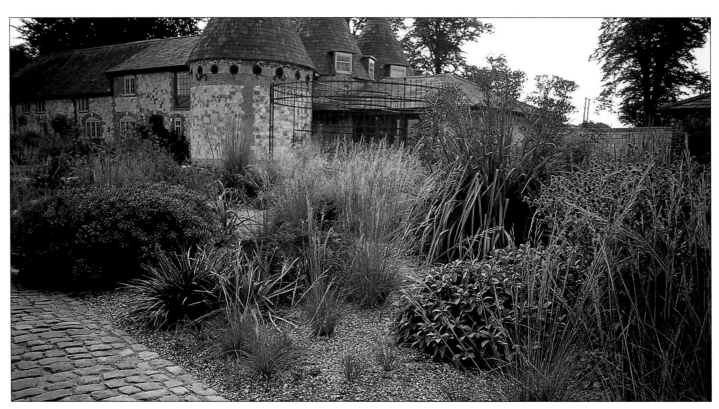

Grasses are excellent for dry gardens. The larger ones create imposing clumps against which the other plants are set.

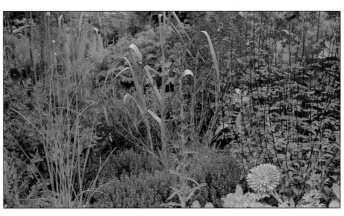

Annuals, such as this marigold (*Calendula*) and vipers bugloss (*Echium vulgare*), will self-sow to provide next year's plants.

This mixed border features plants from regions with a Mediterranean climate. Dry gardens increase the number of plants we can grow.

This is the ultimate dry garden: houseleeks (*Sempervivum*) growing on a house porch. Stonecrops (*Sedum*) also like such a position.

manure are good additives and will improve soil conditions appreciably, especially as they are rich in nutrients. Mulching with organic materials also helps a great deal. A covering of composted bark, for example, will considerably cut down water loss into the atmosphere. It will also gradually become incorporated into the soil, improving the condition. Unfortunately, most dry soils are "hungry", and gardeners need to add material both into the soil and on to its surface on a regular basis.

Living with dry soils

While it is in general terms a good thing to try to improve soil conditions, it is possible to live with them by choosing your plants carefully. Many plants have adapted their demands so that they are able to live with drought or partial drought, particularly plants that come originally from Mediterranean climates. It is very important to choose plants that will tolerate such dry soils. If you try to get ordinary plants to grow in them, you will be disappointed because they will not be able get enough moisture or food from the soil. If, however, you choose plants that have adapted to these conditions, you should have few problems in creating an interesting garden.

Plants for dry conditions

Few gardens have desert conditions, so you don't have to go to extremes and grow only succulents, such as cacti, that tolerate such places. However, there are a lot of plants that come from parts of the world where, for example, dry summers are followed by wet autumns and winters. Many annuals come from these areas, as do bulbs and many silver-leaved plants – try combining these to create an unusual but beautiful garden where their subtle colours are well set off by a gravel background. Weed these areas well, or the effect will be ruined.

Creating a gravel garden

Many gardeners specifically set out to create dry conditions by adding great quantities of gravel to the ordinary soil. This increases its drainage ability and makes it suitable for plants that you may not have been able to grow before.

Damp gardens

The idea of damp gardens conjures up a rather unpleasant image of a garden in which no one would want to linger, but, depending on how the situation is handled, they can be rather beautiful. Apart from anything else, many colours, especially the yellows, stand out so well in gloomy conditions.

What is a damp garden?

A garden can be considered damp in two ways. The first is where the soil is heavy and constantly damp, even though the weather is sunny and bright. The second way can occur near certain coasts. The coastal climate in question is one where the weather is frequently overcast, with rain, drizzle or mist being common, and where, even when it is sunny, the air is still "buoyant" (moving and life-sustaining as opposed to stagnant) and slightly moist, especially under trees. Both are conditions that most gardeners dread, but both can be turned to advantage. Visits to other gardens with similar conditions will soon stimulate you, showing what can be achieved with a bit of determination and a good waterproof jacket.

Aruncus dioicus does best in a moist situation, either in a bed that is moisture-retentive or on the edge of a bog garden.

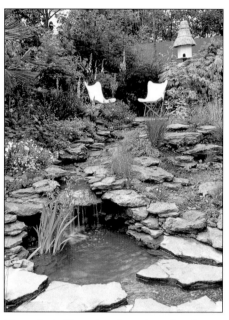

Many plants like a situation where the air never dries out and the soil remains slightly damp, such as along the banks of a stream.

Wet soil

There are two solutions to the problem of wet soils: one is to deal with it and the other is to live with it. In the first case, improving the condition of the soil, especially by adding grit and organic material to it, will help greatly by improving the soil's ability to let the water pass through. Allied to this should be improved drainage. If you simply dig and improve the soil, the bed will fill up with water, held in place by the surrounding poor soil like a sump. You must make certain that the water can drain out of the bed by laying drains either to a soakaway or a nearby ditch. Another possibility is to lead the water to a lower part of the garden, where you can create a pond. Any garden that stays persistently damp should have a proper drainage system installed to get the water away.

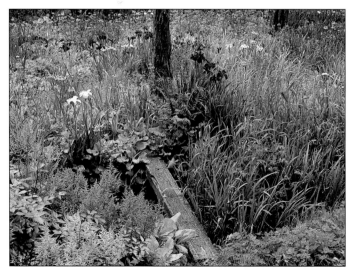

This colourful damp meadow and ditch is full of moisture-loving plants such as candelabra primulas, astilbes and water irises.

A mass of colourful primulas – plants for which a damp position is absolutely ideal. They will self-sow to make this an even better display.

Bog gardens

Living with damp soils is another interesting prospect. The gardener simply has to accept the fact that the soil is always wet and create a bed that is based on plants that like boggy conditions. Fortunately, there are a large number of colourful plants that do like such conditions. If the soil is too heavy, it will help if plenty of well-rotted organic matter is incorporated into it. If there is water actually lying on or just below the surface, this should be removed by laying drains.

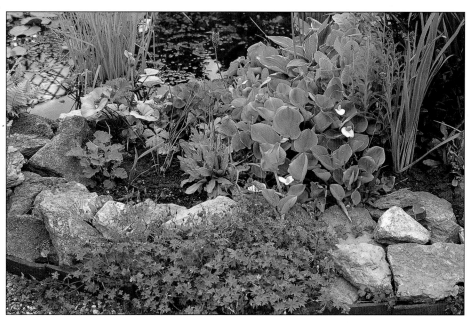

Here a small, damp garden has been built into the edge of a pond. This type of situation really broadens out the range of plants that can be grown.

Creating boggy conditions

While some gardeners go to great expense to get rid of boggy areas, others do the reverse and deliberately create such conditions. One way to do this would be to dig a pond-shaped hole, about 45cm/18in, deep and line it with an old pond liner. Puncturing a few holes in the lowest places will allow excess water to drain away. The hole can then be filled with good soil laced with plenty of well-rotted organic material. The soil should not be allowed to dry out.

Grasses that grow on the damp banks of streams or ponds, hanging their leaves over the water, can look extremely effective.

Damp climate

A damp climate can be a boon if you want to grow plants such as the blue meconopsis, which likes the moist air that reminds it of its Himalayan home. Many other plants do best in a moist, buoyant atmosphere. Primulas and hostas, for example, relish it. In Britain, the maritime climate of Scotland produces some wonderful gardens, growing plants such as primulas, hostas and meconopsis. In many such areas, the soil is surprisingly free-draining. In mountain and hilly areas, for example, the underlying rocks often allow the frequent rain to filter away remarkably quickly, leaving the soil dry. So if there is a prolonged hot spell it is important to water.

Plants for a bog garden

Aconitum napellus	Gunnera manicata	Parnassia palustris
Ajuga reptans	Hemerocallis fulva	Persicaria bistorta
Aruncus dioicus	Hosta	Petasites japonicus var.
Astilbe x arendsii	Iris ensata	giganteus
Astilboides tabularis	Iris orientalis	Primula bulleyana
Astrantia major	Iris sibirica	Primula denticulata
Caltha palustris	Ligularia	Primula florindae
Cardamine pratensis	Lobelia cardinalis	Primula japonica
Cimifuga simplex	Lobelia 'Queen Victoria'	Primula pulverulenta
Darmera peltata	Lobelia siphilitica	Primula vialii
Dierama pulcherimum	Lychnis flos-cuculi	Ranunculus aconitifolius
Dodecatheon meadia	Lysichiton	Rheum palmatum
Eupatorium	Lysimachia nummularia	Rodgersia
Euphorbia griffithii	Lysimachia punctata	Sarracenia purpurea
Euphorbia palustris	Lythrum virgatum	Schizostylis coccinea
Filipendula ulmaria	Meconopsis betonicifolia	Symphytum ibericum
Gentiana asclepiadea	Mimulus cardinalis	Telekia speciosum
Geum rivale	Mimulus lewisii	Trollius

Shady gardens

Like so many other problems in gardening, this one will go away if you make a slight adjustment of attitude and decide to embrace the shade rather than be daunted by it. A visit to any of the big gardens will show shady areas that have been successfully planted, and there is no reason why you should not do the same on a smaller scale.

Coping with shade

For some reason, many people simply ignore the fact that an area is shady and attempt to grow annuals and other sun-loving plants in it. These inevitably languish and frequently die, and the gardeners get very despondent.

There is really no excuse for this problem as a large number of plants are available that actually like shady conditions. Perhaps the colours of these plants might not be so dazzling as the sun-lovers – there are not many bright reds, for example – but they are still colourful enough to put on a good display. Many plants that like shade are yellow, and so stand out well in the gloomy light.

As well as plants with bright flowers, there are many foliage plants that can be used very effectively in such areas. Some have light, variegated or silver-splashed foliage, such as yellow archangel (*Lamium galeobdolon*), which tend to illuminate the darker corners. Others, such as

hostas, have shiny leaves, and these catch and reflect the light, once again helping to brighten up the relative darkness.

Miniature woodlands

Many shade-loving plants grow in woodlands, and they appear, flower, seed and die back all before the trees come into leaf. The absence of leaves above them means that the plants have access to both the sun and the rain. Once the leaves on the trees emerge, the plants die back and remain dormant until the following winter or spring.

These plants, including wood anemones and bluebells, can be planted in a garden in odd pockets

Anemones, here the double *Anemone ranunculoides*, are perfect woodland plants to grow under the shade of shrubs.

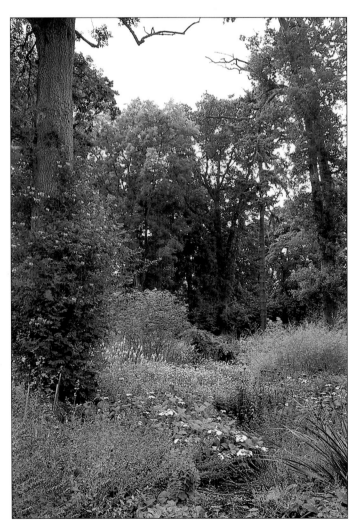

A shady border has been carved out of this mature wood. Here there is sufficient light to grow a wide range of plants.

Even a single tree, such as this quince, is sufficient to create a small woodland garden with a range of plants.

Spring-flowering bulbs, such as these blue scillas, make natural carpets for shady areas. Hellebores are also a very good subject.

of shade, such as under deciduous shrubs. Here, the plants can be seen in spring, but later in the year nothing will grow here because the soil will be covered by the shrub's leaves. This makes good use of space. Several such shrubs, perhaps of varying height and with this type of under-planting, can be used to create a miniature woodland, even in the heart of a town.

Lack of sunlight

The north side of a house (south in the southern hemisphere) is often considered a problem area because of its lack of direct sunlight. Again, it is quite possible to create an

Reducing shade

You can increase the amount of light reaching the plants under trees by removing some of the branches, especially the lower ones. Alternatively, you can thin the branches so that more dappled light reaches the ground. If the trees are listed, then you may have to seek permission before removing any limbs. In basement and other dark patios, the amount of light can be increased by painting walls white to reflect what light there is.

Winter aconites thrive in shade. Give them a moist woodland-type soil with plenty of leaf mould and they will colonize.

effective border there simply by choosing plants that like the shade. Most woodland plants, for example, will grow there.

Dry shade

An area that is both dry and shady is one of the worst problems to cope with because most shade-loving plants are woodland plants, which thrive in a moist, fibre-rich soil. Soils can be improved by adding plenty of well-rotted organic material to them – leaf mould is a natural material to use.

Creating shade

Sometimes it can be a problem if you have no shade in the garden when you want to grow plants such as hellebores, which do not like too much sun. Try building a wooden or metal framework over which you stretch shade-netting, creating nice dappled shade. These structures may not look elegant but they are ideal for their intended purpose. They are also useful for temporarily housing shade-loving plants while bushes or trees become large enough to provide natural shade.

Anemone blanda and hellebores are two good choices to brighten up a patch of light shade.

Some plants for the shade

Alchemilla mollis	Epimedium	Persicaria affinis
Anemone nemorosa	Eranthis hyemalis	Phlox divaricata
Arum italicum	Euphorbia amygdaloides	Phlox stolonifera
Aruncus dioicus	robbiae	Podophyllum peltatum
Bergenia	Geranium	Polygonatum
Brunnera macrophylla	Helleborus	Polystichum setiferum
Caltha palustris	Hosta	Primula
Campanula latifolia	Houttuynia cordata	Pulmonaria
Cardamine	Iris foetidissima	Sanguinaria canadensis
Cardiocrinum giganteum	Kirengshoma	Smilacina
Carex pendula	Lamium galeobdolon	Smyrnium perfoliatum
Clintonia	Lathyrus vernus	Stylophorum
Convallaria majalis	Lilium martagon	Symphytum grandiflorum
Corydalis flexuosa	Liriope muscari	Tellima grandiflora
Dicentra	Meconopsis	Trillium
Digitalis purpurea	Milium effusum 'Aureum'	Uvularia
Dryopteris filix-mas	Myosotis sylvatica	Vancouveria

Small gardens

More and more people are living in houses or apartments that only have small gardens; some, indeed are minute. The keen gardener's heart may sink at such limitations, but it is surprising what you can pack into a small space. As always, it just needs some imagination and determination to create a garden to be proud of.

Packing them in

If you more interested in growing plants than having space in which to sit around or have barbecues, then the amount of hard surfaces or lawn should be reduced to a minimum and as much space as possible devoted to borders. Avoid grass unless you have somewhere to store a lawnmower, because mowers need sheds and sheds take up valuable space.

Although there are recommended planting distances for plants, these, like many rules in gardening, can be ignored and the plants set close together for maximum impact. Some will object and crowd other plants out, but these can be culled totally and replaced by something not so vigorous or kept in place by trimming. Tightly packed plants need to be watered and fed regularly because they are taking a lot of water and nutrients out of the soil.

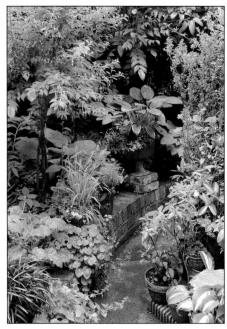

A curved path gives the impression that more garden exists just around the corner. Such illusions make a garden seem much bigger.

One of a kind

Rather than having a drift of one particular plant, as you might in a bigger garden, you should restrict yourself to one plant of each species, otherwise the whole garden could end up with just one or two different types of plant in it. This can make the borders look rather spotty, so drifts can be created using different plants of a similar colour.

The best single plants are those that produce several stems, creating a small clump. Those that produce just a single stem can look rather lost, although there are many such plants, verbascums for example, that make a wonderful accent as they emerge from the surrounding plants. Similarly, a single red poppy can look stunning and will definitely draw the eye.

Foliage plants

A small garden benefits from foliage plants in the same way that large gardens do from grasses. Foliage plants will help to calm down the liveliness of the border and produce somewhere for the eye to rest. This is important in a small garden packed with plants, as the overall appearance can become overly busy. Another use of foliage in any garden, but particularly in a small garden, is to surround a single flowering plant with green or silver leaves so that it makes the flowers stand out, accenting them with a posy effect.

Vertical space

Every bit of space in a small garden is at a premium to a plant-lover, so it is important to remember that a garden is three-dimensional. Climbing plants can be used against walls or fences. It may also be possible to use one or two posts or tripods, if there is space, to add to

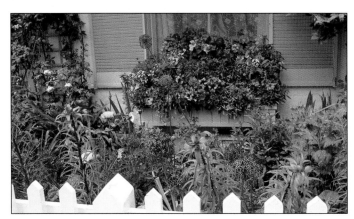

Every inch of space needs to be used to maximum effect in a small garden, including, as here, window sills.

Use containers planted up with annuals and perennials, such as this hosta, to fill out any odd corners.

Plants to cut back

Achillea	Eupatorium
Aconitum	Foeniculum
Aruncus	Helenium
Aster	Rudbeckia
Campanula	Sanguisorba

this vertical accent. As well as climbers, annuals can be used in hanging baskets and window boxes to add colour at or above eye level.

Easy ways to cheat

It is possible to use a few optical tricks to make the garden look bigger. Cover the fences with plants so that the margins of the garden cannot be seen. This trick works particularly well if there is a neighbouring garden with shrubs and other plants peering over the fence, as it will look as if your garden continues. Use a winding path that

Well-planned use of plenty of foliage – so that you cannot see the boundary edges of the garden – is a simple way to make the space feel a great deal larger.

disappears around a corner at the bottom of the garden so that it seems as if your garden continues out of sight. Paler-coloured plants set towards the end of a short garden will deceive the eye and appear farther away than they are.

Large mirrors covering a wall can give the impression that the wall does not exist and the garden carries on, though the mirrors must be angled so that anyone approaching

cannot see their own reflection. Another idea is to erect an arch, which can be covered with climbing plants, just in front of a wall, and then back the arch with a mirror to give the impression that the garden continues under the arch. Similarly, using a *trompe l'oeil* painting on a wall, perhaps a picture of a gate opening into another garden, will deceive viewers into believing that more lies beyond.

Miniaturizing plants

Many taller perennial plants can be made to grow shorter simply by cutting them back to the ground when they have made about 45cm/18in of growth. The plants re-grow but will usually flower when they have obtained only about half their normal height and size.

With imagination and determination, an amazing number of plants can be crammed into a small space.

Even a modest water feature has been fitted into this extremely small garden. Annual and perennial foliage plants help to fill space without making the garden feel cramped.

Large gardens

Most gardeners with large gardens manage to fill them in one way or another, even if involves putting much of the space down to lawns. Large lawns can be elegant, but without children to play on them they can seem a bit excessive, and there are many more interesting things you could do with the space.

Large-scale plantings

Plenty of space means that you can create large-scale plantings, including sweeping herbaceous borders. These are large borders that were traditionally filled only with perennial plants, although these days a number of annuals and even shrubs are often included. The plants are planted in drifts, often with five or more plants in each area, so that the border is "painted" with broad strokes of colour.

It is important that any such borders should be deep as well as long; tall plants in a narrow border rarely work. Try and make the depth of the border twice that of the tallest plants. Two borders often work better than one, and two parallel ones with a grass path between them is ideal. The path should preferably be as wide as the

Having a large garden not only allows you to create lavish bedding displays but also gives plenty of scope for walkways and features such as arches.

borders are deep. Such borders are displayed best if they are grown against a green hedge. Yew is ideal and it is not as slow growing as many people think. A fairly respectable hedge can be achieved in about five years and it will begin to mature at eight.

It is equally possible to use large areas of bedding material, especially if you like to create intricate patterns in colour and texture. There are a number of plants that can be used

for these, some growing to a very even height, while others can be used to vary this or to create accents or focal points. These beds can be laid out directly on the ground, surrounded by lawns, or they can form part of a more complicated plan in which a knot garden of box hedges is created, with the bedding plants used as in-fills. Great fun can be had by creating a low-level maze in this kind of way, using a mixture of paths and beds.

Plenty of space to play with means that passionate gardeners can be creative on a grand scale, as these enormous herbaceous borders show.

As well as straight borders, spacious gardens allow huge, swirling areas of plants that show off their colour and shape to maximum effect.

Large plants

Aruncus	*Helianthus*
Cephalaria	*Heliopsis*
Cimifuga	*Inula magnifica*
Cortaderia	*Lavatera*
Cosmos	*cachemiriana*
Cynara	*Ligularia*
cardunculus	*Macleaya*
Delphinium	*Miscanthus*
Eremurus	*Rheum*
Eupatorium	*Rudbeckia*
purpureum	*laciniata*
Gunnera	*Sanguisorba*
manicata	*Verbascum*

If you have a large space, you can indulge in some of the most impressive plants available. This *Gunnera manicata* is one of the largest perennials used in gardens.

Gardens within gardens

Another good idea for a large garden is to divide it up into a series of smaller gardens. Dividing in this way creates spaces that are more intimate – more like individual rooms than one vast space. This can be effective in country gardens, where the landscape is already expansive and open. Each "room" should be given its own individual character, some formal, some informal, with varied planting. Perhaps one could be a white garden while another could contain only fragrant flowers (a seat would be invaluable in this one).

Large plants

It sounds obvious, but many people forget that a large garden needs large plants, especially if you keep it fairly open. If you have a large pond, then a huge clump of *Gunnera manicata* will look impressive. Great fountains of leaves erupting from large clumps of grasses, such as pampas (*Cortaderia*) or miscanthus, can create focal points at the end of paths or at the bottom of long lawns. They look even better if planted where the evening light shines through them.

Working with a large space

Large gardens that are intensively cultivated can use up a lot of time and a great deal of money, so a large-scale development should be embarked on only if you feel confident that you will have sufficient time. Fortunately, time can often offset costs, because you can propagate all your own material rather than buying it, but a large garden almost always needs a lot of plants to work really successfully.

Finally, the wind is a factor that cannot be forgotten in large gardens, especially where tall plants are likely to be grown in clumps, with nothing behind or in front to protect them from being blown over. A windbreak could be created around the garden, and plants staked if necessary.

Although shrubs are another topic altogether, it is worth saying here that they can be very useful in large gardens, as providers of valuable wind protection.

Family gardens

Keen gardeners who start a family quickly discover that neat gardens and active children do not often mix. Since there is no point trying to stop the children using the garden, or constantly telling them to get off this area and not touch that plant, a compromise is needed whereby everyone can live happily. Remember that a garden should be a fun place for everyone.

Children in the garden

Whatever you do, children will always be children, and quite rightly so. They will want to play ball and racket games in the garden, and will want to career around on bikes and in go-karts. These things present problems for the gardener – balls will crash through the borders, bringing down plants; cyclists or go-karters will veer off the lawn or path and end up lying in a nest of tangled plants.

In the ideal family garden there should be plenty of space and a range of provisions, so everybody is able to relax and play in their own way.

Play space

To some extent, trouble can be avoided by creating a family garden where there is room for all activities. Plenty of lawn or hard surface should be provided on which children can play. There could also be special areas for them, perhaps with swings, sandpits, "camps" or "houses". The very best gardens are those with a variety of nooks and crannies in which children can hide, so, if possible, you could try creating some of these.

If you can, provide as much lawn area as possible – for children to play without falling on hard surfaces or wreaking havoc in the borders.

Some features can be built with the future in mind. This sand pit, for example, can eventually be turned into a water feature.

Easy plants for children to grow

Antirrhinum	Lobelia
Calendula	Tagetes
Helianthus	Thunbergia alata
annuus	Tropaeolum
Lathyrus odoratus	majus

Separate rooms

Your garden may be large enough for you to divide it up into a number of areas, each for a particular activity. This may, for example, include an area for playthings as well as a place for growing precious plants.

Children's gardens

Many young children are very keen on gardening – they love to see things growing. Although eager to help you with your gardening, most children are happiest of all with a small plot of their own. Encourage them to grow annuals, which are quick to germinate and produce colourful results of which they can be justifiably proud. A small selection of quick-growing vegetables will also delight. Children's interests can wane as rapidly as they began, so be prepared to absorb the plot back into the garden. Alternatively, provide them with long-flowering plants, such as *Tagetes*, which will fill the space over a long period.

Tough lawns

The family lawn can take quite a beating and it will be impossible to keep it perfectly pristine. Instead of using the soft grasses that would be needed for a high-quality lawn, use some of the tougher species, which will stand the considerable wear and tear of family life. These can be used singly or as mixtures of one or more species. Once the family has grown up, you can then switch to a better-quality grass.

Tough grass seed for lawns

Axonopus (carpet grass)
Eremochloa ophiuroides (centipede grass)
Lolium perenne (perennial ryegrass)
Paspalum notatum (bahia grass)
Poa pratensis (Kentucky blue grass)

Pets

Cats, dogs and other pets are also part of the family, and friction can often erupt when they flatten plants or dig up borders. Low fences can deter them from running into borders, but with some dogs it will be necessary to fence off your flower garden completely. Wild birds that you feed in winter also need to be taken into account, as they will often strip plants of flowers or berries that you want to keep. There is little you can do about this except grow plants that they do not touch (skimmia berries, for example, are rarely eaten) or cover plants with a network of dark cotton.

Dining out

It is not only children who indulge in non-gardening pursuits. Most of the family want to do other things at some time or other, and space for relaxing is very important. This may just involve a spot for sitting or for lounging in the sun, or more likely will also include some provision for eating, possibly with a barbecue area.

It is a good idea to surround places where you relax with fragrant plants. These will be most welcome if you sit outside in the evening once the sun has gone down. Remember that certain blues and whites show up especially well in the fading light, so try to use plants with flowers of these colours. In a barbecue area, grow a few herbs so that they can be easily picked and used.

Always provide plenty of space and facilities for relaxation. After all, that is one of the prime functions of a garden.

Special ways with annuals and perennials

If you have a big garden, and plenty of free time at your disposal, then you can indulge in just about every aspect of gardening. However, if you do not have these luxuries, you may well find that you have the space to do only one thing properly, and so you specialize. Alternatively, you may want to garden for just one particular purpose, such as providing cut flowers for your home or local community centre.

There are many ways in which you can specialize, and a few are suggested here. It is possible, for example, to have a border or even a whole small garden devoted to plants that include your name. There are over 100 plants that contain the name Helen, for example, including *Aster novi-belgii* 'Helen' and *Dianthus* 'Helen'. You could create a garden filled with plants mentioned in the works of Shakespeare, or in books by your favourite novelist. Research is involved here, of course, but this kind is usually very enjoyable. In any case, rather than devote a whole garden to any of these themes, you could restrict yourself to just a single border or an area within the main garden. The possibilities are endless and the result is likely to be a unique garden that no one else will have.

Borders can be restricted to one colour or a group of colours. In this scheme, yellows are predominant, but a sprinkling of hot reds has been added to provide some interest.

Fragrant gardens

When thinking of flowers, one's first thoughts normally concern their colour. One of their most important qualities as far as many gardeners are concerned, however, is their smell. Most people have evocative childhood memories of particular flower fragrances, usually associated with a specific garden – often a grandparent's.

Scents

There is nothing quite like the scent of a garden on a summer's day, particularly if associated with the drowsy hum of bees and the fluttering of butterflies. Generally, a warm, sunny day brings out the scents, but there are some that are much more noticeable during or after rain. Scent in a flower is a bonus as far as we are concerned, but nature imbued flowers with it for a reason: to attract pollinators. For this reason, many winter flowers are sweet-smelling. There are not many pollinators around at that time of year and so the flowers have to work particularly hard to attract them.

Some plants throw out their scent with gay abandon and can be smelt at large distances. Others are much more discreet, and you have to put your nose almost into them before the fragrance is detectable. Many of the latter are more apparent once they have been picked and placed in a warm room. Some are only noticeable during the evening as the light fades. Presumably these attract night-flying moths.

The fragrant garden

Not all the plants should be fragrant, or they will become too overpowering and you will be unable to differentiate between the conflicting scents. Place scented plants at key points around the

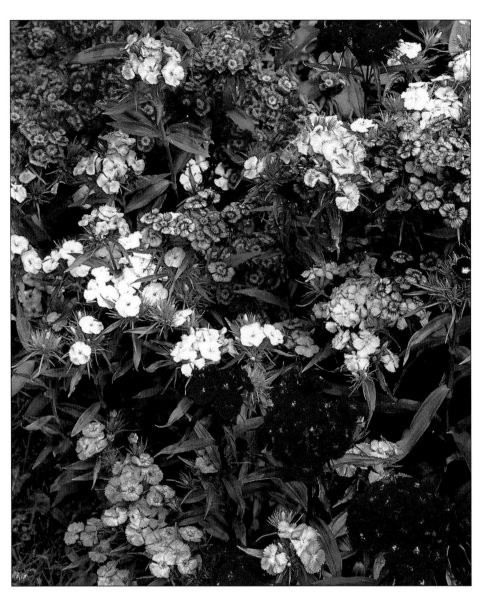

Sweet Williams, *Dianthus barbatus*, have a very distinctive smell – the kind of smell that often triggers memories such as a garden from your childhood.

Placing fragrant flowers near to a window will often flood the rooms beyond with a wonderful scent, especially on warm, balmy summer evenings.

Plants with scented foliage

Agastache
Anthemis punctata cupaniana
Artemisia
Melittis melissophylum
Mentha
Meum athamanticum
Morina longifolia
Nepeta
Pelargonium graveolens
Perovskia atriplicifolia
Salvia

Scents to avoid

Not all plants emit a pleasant scent, and some, such as those that attract flies as pollinators, are downright putrid. However attractive the flowers, *Dracunculus vulgaris*, for example, is not a plant to place near the house. Other cases are not quite so clear cut. Examples such as *Phuopsis stylosa* or *Lilium pyrenaicum* smell of foxes, which some people find repulsive, while others find it mildly attractive.

Many pelargoniums have scented foliage, with the fragrances offered by different varieties ranging from citrus fruits and rose to nutmeg.

garden so that there is the impression that the whole garden is perfumed. Also, try if possible to get a spread of plants so that there are scents throughout the seasons, including winter.

Scent-testing

Try to smell your plants before you acquire them, as some may not be as scented as you wish. Breeders of flowers went through a long period when smell was low down on their list of priorities when creating new plants. Thus many modern sweet peas are not sweet at all: they are scentless. Similarly, many modern pinks are without scent.

Another reason for trying out scents, either in other gardens or at the point of sale, is that you may not like the fragrance of some plants: they may be too sweet and sickly or they may bring back certain unpleasant memories.

Siting fragrant flowers

Fragrant flowers can be placed anywhere you like in the garden, but there are some situations where they are a must. One of the best positions is near places where you sit and relax, as soothing scents will help to recharge your batteries.

Another good place is near windows or doors, so that the scent wafts into the house when the flowers open during a warm day or evening.

Placing fragrant plants next to the driveway, so that you notice them as you get out of the car, is a wonderful way of indicating to the senses that you have arrived home after work, and certainly helps you to relax.

Fragrant foliage

It is not only flowers that can be scented: a lot of plant foliage is too. In some cases, as with flowers, warmth brings out the fragrance, but in most cases the leaves or stems have to be crushed in order to release it. In extreme cases, such as lawn chamomile, *Chamaemelum nobile* 'Treneague', or thyme, the plants are best placed under foot, so that as you walk on them you send up clouds of scent. With most fragrantly foliaged plants, however, it is best to site them near to a path, so that you can run your fingers through them as you walk by.

Pinks (*Dianthus*), both the annual and perennial types, provide a distinctively old-fashioned fragrance to borders. Here, the plant used is *D.* 'Doris'.

Colour gardens

All plants are coloured, so what is a "colour" garden? Well, some gardeners like to use particular colour schemes, choosing either all pastel or all bright colours, for example, rather than just dotting colour around the garden at random. A favourite idea is to create a border or even a whole garden of a single colour – a particularly popular choice being white.

Choosing colours

We all know what colours are, although we may see them slightly differently. What we don't all agree on is which colours are pleasing and which are not. Inevitably, because we are all different, our feelings about certain colours or combinations vary dramatically. Therefore, although there may seem to be codes or formulas for colour use, it is important to do what pleases you; after all, the garden is for you. For a long time, mixing oranges and purples would have been deemed one of the worst sins in gardening, but now influential gardeners are much more adventurous and many will readily combine these colours.

Arranging colours

Using colours in drifts can make a big impact in a garden, and if the drifts are planted so that they merge

Here an exciting, vibrant border has been created, composed entirely of a well-selected range of hot colours such as golds, oranges and reds. These sorts of colours make us feel energetic and dynamic, so they may not be the best choice for a corner where you go to unwind.

harmoniously rather than jump suddenly from one extreme to another, then so much the better. In this way mauves might merge into blues, and yellows into oranges, creating a soft, fluid design that leads the eye around the garden.

If you want to create something more eye-catching, then try planting contrasting colours such as orange and mauve together. If you are not brave enough to put them right next to each other, use a foliage plant between them to soften the impact. As with so many other aspects of designing gardens, it is best to see how other people use colour and then follow those ideas that you like.

Creating different moods

Colours can have a significant effect on our mood. Hot colours such as oranges and flame reds are lively and exciting, whereas the lighter pastel colours are cool and soothing. Dark purples are sombre and heavy and, if overdone in a garden, can produce a leaden appearance.

Single-colour gardens

Experimental gardeners can have great fun by devoting a border or even a whole garden to a single bloom colour – white is an especially popular choice. Such gardens are not truly just one colour anyway, because you have to take the foliage into account. So, a "white" garden is usually made up of white, green and perhaps silver and grey. Even the white may vary from a creamy or a yellowish white to bluish-white, and it takes a fair amount of skill to balance these different variations.

Contrasting colours can make a bold visual statement. These pinkish-orange dahlias stand out vividly against the deep blue salvias.

Soft, pastel colours can create a tranquil, peaceful feeling. Here, pink alliums mix with white geraniums and blue salvias.

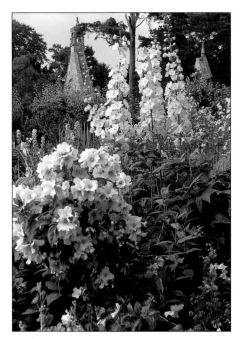

A border devoted to white flowers creates a very peaceful atmosphere. Surprisingly, using just one colour need never be boring.

White flowers

Achillea ptarmica	*Digitalis purpurea* 'Alba'	*Nicotiana sylvestris*
Anaphalis margaritacea	*Epilobium angustifolium*	*Omphalodes linifolia*
Anemone x hybrida	'Album'	*Osteospermum* 'Whirligig'
'Honorine Jobert'	*Geranium sanguineum*	*Paeonia*
Anemone nemorosa	'Album'	*Penstemon* 'White Bedder'
Antirrhinum majus	*Gypsophila paniculata*	*Petunia*
Argyranthemum frutescens	*Iberis sempervirens*	*Phlox paniculata* 'Fujiama'
Bellis	*Lamium maculatum* 'White	*Polygonatum x hybridum*
Campanula latiloba alba	Nancy'	*Ranunculus aconitifolius*
Convallaria majalis	*Lathyrus*	*Romneya coulteri*
Crambe cordifolia	*Leucanthemum* 'Everest'	*Smilacina*
Dianthus	*Lilium*	*Viola*
Dicentra spectabile 'Alba'	*Lysimachia clethroides*	*Zantedeschia aethiopica*

Two-colour gardens

This variation on the single-colour planting idea involves a border, or whole garden, being planted with two different colours. White and gold or yellow and blue are two popular and pleasing combinations. The two colours can be equal in quantity or mainly one with a touch of the other as a contrast.

Hot colours

Vibrant and exciting bright orange, flame red and orange-yellow can be great fun to play with. They attract the eye and can create a focal point in the garden. But, like parties, they are great fun once in a while but can lose their appeal if done to excess. Certainly, a whole garden planted in these colours would become tiring after a short while, so it is better to create just one border or a part of a border, placing them in key positions. They can also look effective on the far side of a pond.

Contrasting colours

Using colours that contrast particularly boldly with each other can add drama to a border and will draw the eye. Many people find that some contrasting colours are more acceptable than others. Most would agree that bright red looks fabulous with green, for example, but they may be more reserved about other combinations, such as orange with purple. As with hot colours, gardeners should always bear in mind that dramatic contrasts can begin to jar if used too much.

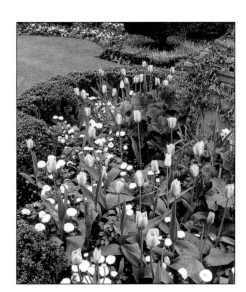

You can create a white garden in spring, as seen here, and then change the plants to have a "hot" red garden in the summer.

The hotter colours may be dramatic and thrilling, but remember that even excitement can become boring if it is overdone, and you certainly don't want to produce something that amounts to a visual assault. Restricting bold colours to one border is often much more pleasing.

Water gardens

Water has been one of the basic building blocks of decorative gardens since gardens first began. Whether it is still or moving, it has a calming tranquillity about it that sums up the essence of a garden. Water can be used in a wide variety of ways, including features that are suitable for the smaller garden.

What are water features?

There is a wide range of possibilities for using water in the garden, ranging from lakes in big ones to just a dustbin lid full of water in a small one. Water can be used in the form of a static pond or pool, or it can be used as a stream, with all the movement that implies. Streams can involve cascades, waterfalls and pools, and can become a striking feature of the garden. It is also possible to use water in such a way that there is no standing water at all, just water seeping between fixed pebbles.

All these possibilities can involve plants in one way or another, allowing you to use plants and to create effects that a garden without water cannot achieve.

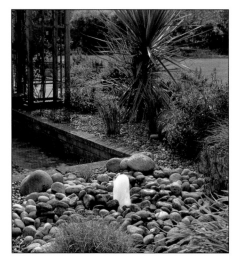

Water features do not need to contain any standing water. Here, bubble fountains give sound and image without the dangers.

Areas of contrast

Water complements the plants in a garden beautifully. It can create tranquil, reflective areas as a contrast to some lively planting, or it can bustle along in a stream, in contrast to the static plants, creating a sparkling streak of silver. Water can also produce noise, such as the tinkling of a fountain or the more regular pouring of a waterspout. The movement of water in a stream can also be very soothing to watch.

Wildlife

One of the many reasons why gardeners like ponds and other water features in their gardens is that they attract wildlife. They produce a source of drinking and bathing water for a large number of birds and insects, and ponds can also attract toads. Other animals, especially nocturnal ones, may drink from a pond at night. Such wildlife is attracted not only to the water but also to the plants that surround it, which furnish them with valuable cover and food.

Plants and water

One of the advantages of having a water feature is that it lets you extend the range of plants featured in your garden to include those that enjoy growing in or around water.

Some plants, such as water lilies, thrive in the deep water itself, while others prefer the shallow water margins, where they can get their roots down into the mud. Other plants like the muddy edges of a pond, where they are generally out of

Different types of garden can always be combined. This is a water garden where colour effects have also been created – using flowers in gold and white.

You can create water gardens on a modest scale, as this stream and pool demonstrate.

Water allows the gardener to use plants that cannot be grown in any other way. These water lilies are a prime example.

Waterside plants

Aruncus	Lysichiton
Astilbe	Lysimachia
Caltha	Lythrum
Cardamine	Mimulus
Cimifuga	Onoclea sensibilis
Darmera peltata	Osmunda regalis
Eupatorum	Peltiphyllum
Filipendula	peltatum
Gunnera	Persicaria
Hosta	bistorta
Iris ensata	Phragmites
Iris sibirica	Primula
Ligularia	Rheum
Lobelia	Rodgersia
cardinallis	Trollius

the water but where their roots are occasionally submerged. Another group, such as hostas and rodgersias, like the area next to the pond, which is out of water but still damp, while mimulus and many primulas relish being planted beside a stream, where they are occasionally splashed and where the air is nice and buoyant. The range of plants within all these different groups is enormous.

Bog gardens

Many of the plants that like growing on the margins of ponds can be grown to really great effect in a bog garden. This is commonly defined as an area that has a great deal of moisture-retaining humus in the soil, so that it never dries out, though this does not mean that it has to be squelchy. If, for any reason, you want to get rid of a pond, rather than filling it in you can simply puncture the lining so that the water drains away, and then fill it up with some fibrous material to make your perfect bog garden.

Safety

Water can be dangerous, especially to young children, so very careful thought must be given before you start to dig deep holes in your garden for ponds of any kind. There are various attractive compromises. It is possible to create relatively safe features in which water bubbles out of, say, a rock and then disappears between fixed stones into a safe underground reservoir. This idea leaves no surface water, which can prove to be dangerous.

A pond can be especially appealing if it is designed so that it blends in with the rest of the garden, adding to the overall scene rather than being a totally separate feature. Placing water features where they are "discovered" as something of a surprise also adds a delightful touch.

Specialist flower gardens

The majority of people grow plants in order to create an attractive garden in which they can relax and enjoy themselves. Others, however, do so because they simply enjoy the process of growing plants or even need to grow plants. In the latter cases, the actual appearance of the garden will be of less importance than the plants it produces.

Cut flowers

These are an important part of many people's lives. Most gardeners cut a few flowers for the house, but some grow plants especially for that very purpose, devoting part or even all of the garden to producing them. Rows of flowering sweet peas or plants with attractive foliage such as hostas are their common fare. Most people don't need to have their whole garden turned over to the production of flowers for cutting, but some gardeners enjoy providing displays for churches or hospitals or even selling them at local markets.

For them it is important to know which plants can be used as cut stems and which last longest in water. There are many old favourites, but it is often exciting to discover new ones from the vast range of plants that gardeners have at their beck and call, so it is always worth experimenting. Buy one plant of something that might be suitable. Try it and, if it works, propagate it so that you have a row of unusual material.

The average gardener does not want to devote the whole garden to cut flowers and probably doesn't have room for even a border of such things. It is, however, easy to incorporate a number of plants for cutting among the other plants in the borders. Wigwams of sweet peas, for example, look good as well as providing cut material.

Sweet peas are typically grown for exhibition and cut flower purposes and need not be grown in the main decorative beds.

Phlox makes an excellent cut flower. As well as being grown in special beds for cutting, phlox is a good choice for borders.

Flower shows

There is a long tradition, especially among cottage gardeners, of growing plants for exhibition. Most tend these days to be local affairs, where there are mixed shows, but there are still a number of local and national shows that are devoted in whole or in part to one type of flower. Thus sweet peas, chrysanthemums and dahlias are still popular with exhibitors. Pinks (*Dianthus*), auriculas, and irises are also still shown fairly extensively.

These plants can be grown in the general borders, but growing them in separate beds, albeit more practical than attractive, means that the gardener can tend them easily and bring them on to their very best.

Specialist growers

Some gardeners are interested in particular plants, often to the exclusion of others. They may grow them as part of a decorative garden or they may grow them in special beds designed to suit their particular plants. Examples of some of the more popular groups of plants for growing in general beds are hellebores, geraniums and hostas.

Some collectors with large collections, however, grow them in beds devoted to their specialization. These plants will often need special growing conditions, and so lovers of alpine plants will construct special raised beds where the soil is very free-draining, while those interested in hellebores may well construct shade beds made with wooden frames covered with shade netting. These may not be the most elegant of gardens, but they serve the purpose for which the gardener requires them and certainly suit the needs of the plants, as the conditions are tailor made for them.

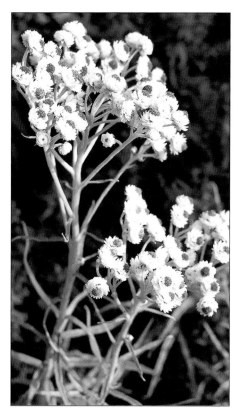

There are many flowers in the garden that can be cut for drying. This perennial, *Anaphalis nepalenis*, is just one good example.

Small nurseries

There are certain gardeners who get so passionate about plants that they are not content with the confines of their own garden and may want to start growing them for everybody else as well. What might have started out as a conventional garden soon turns into a small nursery. Frequently, such a garden will contain plants planted randomly in stock beds, so that they are readily available for propagation. It will also contain lots of plants grown in pots, ready for sale.

Other ways of gardening

None of these types of gardens may be conventional but they are certainly all perfectly worthwhile ways of gardening. There are undoubtedly many people who gain a great deal of enjoyment from these kinds of specialist approaches.

Most specialist gardeners are likely to have started out simply by devoting a relatively small plot to their purpose until enthusiasm has really taken over. Such specialization can be exciting and if you succumb you will come to know a great deal about plants.

Growing rare plants

As mentioned before, there are other gardeners who are not especially interested in gardens as such; they are really only interested in growing plants. While they may not specialize in any particular genus or family, they get their enjoyment from growing unusual and rare plants.

One of the reasons that some plants are rare in gardens is straightforward – they are very difficult to grow. This presents a challenge to certain gardeners, who will spend a lot of time making certain that the conditions are just right and giving nurturing attention to individual plants, much more than would be given to normal ones. Many people find this a particularly exciting form of gardening.

Flowers for cutting

Acanthus	Delphiniums
Achillea	Eryngium
Alstroemeria	Gypsophila
Aster	Heliopsis
Callistephus	Lathyrus odoratus
chinensis	Liatris
Chrysanthemum	Molucella
Convallaria majalis	Physalis
Dahlia	Rudbeckia
Dianthus	Solidago

Bear in mind that if you want to produce larger flowers, such as the delphiniums shown here, primarily for cutting purposes, then it may be best to grow them in separate beds, as cutting from a decorative bed will leave big gaps.

Container gardens

While most traditional gardens consist of beds, with possibly areas of lawn or hard surface, it is possible to have a garden without these. It is even possible to have a garden on a balcony or rooftop without any access to a conventional garden. The secret? Containers.

What are containers?

Plants can be grown in any form of container, from a small yogurt carton to a large terracotta pot. Pots made of plastic or ceramic, as well as wooden barrels and tubs, are frequently used, and there has been an increase in the popularity of metal containers. Although virtually any container can be used to contain plants, it is important to remember the dignity of the plant and avoid planting it in something completely unsuitable. A plastic tub with the name of the product it once contained still on the side, for example, does the plant no favours.

Containers come in a number of forms. The obvious one is a round pot, varying in size from a small terracotta pot to a large ceramic one.

An unusual container of perennial plants. These cowslips (*Primula veris*) and violas provide the perfect colourful and informal combination for this basket.

Wood is frequently used to construct boxes of various types, including large square Versailles tubs and rectangular window boxes. Containers can also come in the form of baskets. Ordinary willow baskets can be stood on the ground, hiding a lesser container within them, but more usually they are made of metal or plastic and are used as hanging containers.

Where to use containers

Containers can be used anywhere in the garden and are particularly useful for people who have no proper beds or borders. They can be placed on the ground, stood on plinths or walls, hung from poles or walls or stood on balconies and roof gardens.

Pots can be used singly as focal points placed at the end of paths or on the top of steps. A large,

Containers can be seasonal, such as this lovely spring bouquet of primroses and violets. Plants from these containers can be planted out in the garden after flowering.

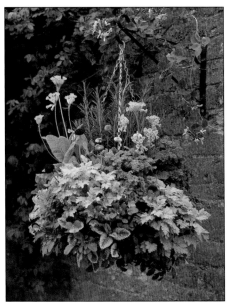

Perennials can even be used in hanging baskets. Violas, cowslips, and feverfew feature here.

Containers need not be filled with flowering colour, as these foliage plants show. Grasses are particularly successful container choices.

A collection of pots can be used as a substitute for a border in a small garden. To change the design, all you need do is move the pots around.

stunning pot containing a plant with good architectural qualities will certainly draw the eye.

Used in pairs, pots make good punctuation points when placed on either side of gateways, archways or other entrances. A pair of terracotta pots containing standard box trees on either side of a front door can transform the entrance into something very stylish. Similarly, a pair of pots on either side of the bottom or top of a flight of stairs is very effective.

When arranged in groups, pots tend to look best if they are different sizes, especially if the plants at the back are taller than those at the front. In formal gardens, a series of containers with similar content can be placed at intervals down a path or around a pool.

Mobility

Pots can be moved around the garden, giving you the opportunity to change the scene throughout the seasons. Plants that are out of flower can be tucked away and brought out when the blooms break open. They can also be moved into areas of a border or bed that happen to be rather dull at the time. Large pots are very heavy once full of soil, so it is important to get help when moving them.

Container plants

A wide range of plants can be used in containers. In fact, virtually any plant is suitable, although those with long taproots tend to be unhappy unless the pot is really deep.

Some plants are used almost exclusively in containers. Trailing plants, for example, have been bred especially for hanging baskets and window boxes. Although annuals are the most popular for temporary baskets, which last for only one season, perennials can be useful for

more permanent settings. Many, such as agapanthus, are flowering, but some, such as hostas and ferns, are used as foliage plants to add substance to any grouping of pots.

Colour in a pot

Containers can be used to add gaiety to a scene, and these are usually bursting with bright colours. There is no reason, however, why the colours should not be more subdued and subtle. A container with a single colour can frequently be more effective than one with many colours, and the colours can be combined by grouping the pots.

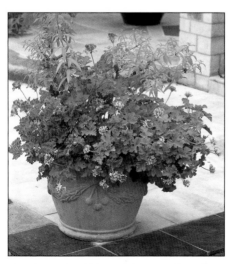

Containers do not have to be complicated creations. Here, a couple of pelargoniums give plenty of foliage and flower interest.

Plants for containers

Agapanthus	Hosta
Ageratum	Impatiens
Alonsoa	Lobelia
Argyranthemum	Nemisia
Begonia	Pelargonium
Bellis	Petunia
Bidens ferulifolia	Phormium
Brachycome	Primula
iberidifolia	Senecio cinerea
Cordyline	Tagetes
australis	Tropaeolum
Diascia	Verbena x
Felicia amelloides	hybrida
Helichrysum	Viola x
petiolare	wittrockiana

Plants with a purpose

Many people come to gardening with the sole intention of keeping the space around the house tidy. Gradually they begin to realize that there can be more to it than that, and that great enjoyment can be had from creating an attractive space in which the plants play an important part.

Initial gardening attempts often tend to be lacking in unity, with donations from friends and neighbours and the occasional plant from a garden centre dotted around. Eventually, however, you realize that the best effect is created by thinking of the garden as a whole and planning it as a complete picture.

The backbone to this picture is the plants. At first, plants seem to be no more than a series of flower colours and shapes – but gradually, as you get deeper into gardening, you will become more aware of the different groups of plants and how they can be used most effectively in different circumstances. In this section we look at four of these groups. The differences are fairly obvious when you think about them, but they can be overlooked when you are planning a garden, particularly if colour has a dominant place in your mind. But, as you will discover, there is a lot more to plants than just colour.

This combination of foliage and flowering plants creates an interest that is far greater than if the two types were used separately.

Foliage plants

From a gardener's point of view, the foliage should have an equal importance to the flowers. After all, if you take away the leaves, the flowers would be lost – their colours would not have anywhere near the impact they do when surrounded by foliage.

Colour

Few people would disagree with the statement that leaves are green. But is it that simple? The first impression when looking at a garden is that most leaves certainly are green, but a closer look reveals an incredible range of greens, from pale to very dark green and often with touches of yellow or blue in them. Further variety is added by whether the leaves are shiny or dull. Dull leaves tend not to stand out, while shiny leaves add sparkle to the border, especially in shady places, where they shine out as they catch odd shafts of light.

Further examination of the borders will show that many leaves are not, in fact, green at all. A quick

This curious, little-grown annual, *Medicago echinus*, has a distinctive colour pattern that makes it perfect for borders.

survey will reveal quite a number of plants that have silver, grey, purple and yellow foliage. There are even small quantities of red-, black- and blue-leaved plants as well. This wide spectrum of leaf colour means that a great deal of variety can be created in a garden without even taking account of any flowers.

Variegation

Many plants have leaves that are more than one colour. The most common variegations are based on green and yellow – some yellows so pale as to be almost white, with others tending towards orange, and

all the variations between. Some plants have more than two colours. *Houttuynia cordata* 'Chameleon', for example, has foliage in green, brownish-red and yellow.

Variegated foliage is in itself very attractive, but can be too busy to the eye if overused and does not always make a good background for flower colour. However, it is wonderful for lightening a dark corner, where the yellows really stand out.

Other leaf qualities

The texture and shape of leaves are also important aspects to take into account when creating a picture.

Plants with variegated foliage

Acorus calamus 'Variegatus'
Aquilegia vulgaris 'Woodside'
Arum italicum 'Pictum'
Astrantia major 'Sunningdale Variegated'
Brunnera macrophylla 'Hadspen Cream'
Convallaria majalis 'Variegata'
Cortaderia selloana 'Gold Band'
Eryngium bourgatii
Euphorbia marginata (a)
Fragaria x *ananassa* 'Variegata'
Hakononechloa macra 'Aureola'
Hosta
Iris pallida 'Variegata'
Lamium maculatum
Miscanthus sinensis 'Zebrinus'
Myosotis scorpioides 'Maytime'
Osteospermum 'Jewel'
Phalaris arunindinacea 'Picta'
Phlox paniculata 'Harlequin'
Phlox paniculata 'Nora Leigh'
Phlox paniculata 'Pink Posie'
Phormium tenax 'Sundowner'
Pleioblastus auricomus
Pulmonaria saccharata
Silybum marianum
Sisyrinchium striatum 'Aunt May'
Symphytum x *uplandicum* 'Variegatum'
Tanacetum vulgare 'Silver Lace'

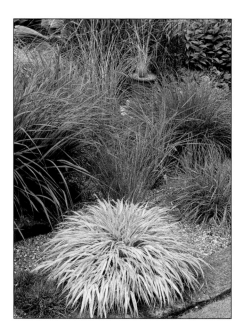
The texture, shape and colour of grasses well repay their use in the garden, especially when combined in this kind of way.

The play of light on plants is very important in a well-designed garden. Here, evening light rakes across *Crocosmia masoniorum* leaves.

Pulmonarias are grown as flowering plants for spring, but if they are cut back after flowering, the new foliage will remain fresh throughout the summer.

Prickly foliage may make a plant difficult to weed around, but it does provide a contrast to the surrounding leaves.

The texture can be velvety, rough or smooth. A velvety texture gives the plant interest, and the tiny hairs that give the feeling of velvet can add a greyish-white bloom to the leaves. Rough leaves may often be dull, whereas smooth leaves are frequently shiny and bright.

The shape is very important. Some plants have long, spiky leaves, while others can be almost round, with or without lobes and/or serrations, with lots of variations in between these two extremes. A mixture of shapes makes a border more interesting, especially when contrasting shapes are used. On the other hand, using plants with leaves of the same shape can make the border more calming and tranquil, though there is inevitably an inherent danger of also making it more boring.

Foliage as a background

While an eye-catching garden can be created entirely out of interesting foliage, it is more common to use a combination of foliage and flowers to create your composition. Most borders consist of a mixture of plants grown specifically for their foliage and other foliage plants that provide an especially effective backdrop for the flowers.

Green will act as the perfect background to most colours, but works particularly well with its complementary colour, red. Silver works well with softer colours, although a bright red or magenta will stand out beautifully against it. Purple is a difficult colour as a background, as it can become very leaden if used in excess, but it works well with contrasting orange and flame colours.

Foliage as foliage

Leaves are quite capable of being a feature on their own. There may not be such a wide variety of foliage colours as there are for flowers, but there are still enough to paint a picture solely made up of leaves, especially when taking shape and texture into account too.

One advantage of a purely foliage garden is that it has a much longer season than one devoted to flowers. In fact, if you take evergreen plants into account, the foliage garden is always in season. However, most plants flower at some point, so few gardens are devoted entirely to foliage, though some foliage purists cut off flower stems as they appear.

Foliage works particularly well in shady or woodland-type areas, and the addition of some variegated foliage here and there will add welcome touches of lightness.

A border devoted to silver foliage works well, but most silver-leaved plants grow only in sunny situations, so you will need to plan your borders accordingly.

Ferns are superb foliage plants to use in shady positions. They act as a brilliant foil for flowering plants.

Dramatic effects can often be created if interesting or bold shapes are used, as in these sword-like leaves.

Differently shaped plants

Some plants have such a dominant shape that they are always bound to catch the eye. A great fountain of pampas grass (*Cortaderia*) is a good example, or the jagged candelabra of the giant biennial Scotch thistle (*Onopordum*), which towers above the viewer. These spectacular plants are invaluable in the garden as focal points, since they catch the eye.

Architectural plants – those with usefully sculptural shapes – can be placed in a border to heighten its interest or in places such as at the end of a path or the end of the garden, often in splendid isolation. They can be planted in the ground or in pots. Either way, they act as living sculptures and provide features that immediately attract the eye.

Such plants work well in a formal garden, used singly as centrepieces or planted at intervals along either a path or border to give a sense of rhythm. Sometimes large plants are necessary to complete the scene. For example, the giant leaves of *Gunnera*

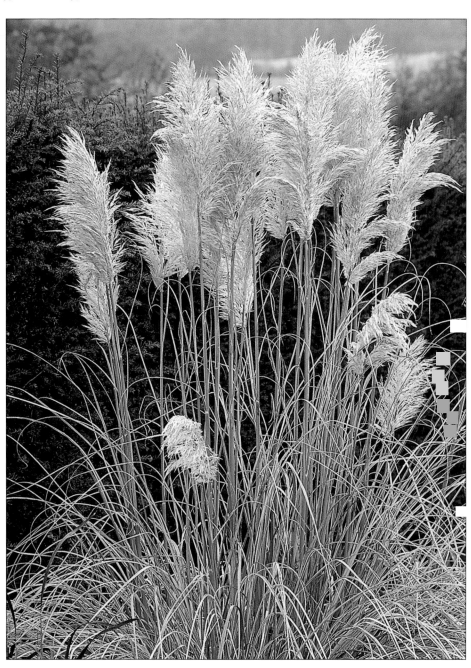

The ever-popular pampas grass, *Cortaderia*, is a particularly stately plant and is extremely eye-catching, whether grown by itself or as part of a border.

Salvia sclarea's upright nature makes it, quite literally, stand out in the crowd, creating a focal point in this border.

manicata look perfect beside a large pond, while not many garden sights can better a stand of *Stipa gigantea* set by itself where the evening sun can shine through its leaves.

A vast choice of shapes

Next time you visit a large garden, take a look at the wide variety of shapes there are among the plants. Some are tall and thin, others are flat and mat-like. In some the leaves

erupt like a fountain, while in others the foliage forms a tight clump, frequently in rounded hummocks, perhaps even a ball. All these different shapes can be used to great advantage to give variation within the bed or border.

Close-up shots of flowers on packets of seeds or on pot labels usually show the flower in detail but rarely the whole plant. You need to check the plant out, either in a book

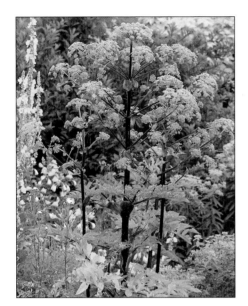

The tall stems and rounded flower heads of this angelica create a distinctive, cloud-like image in the border that sets it apart.

or by looking at it in another garden, to see what shape it will have. The shape of the flowers, and their colour, can also add to a plant's architectural quality. *Liatris*, for example, erupts like fireworks, while *Limnanthes* forms a carpet.

Working with plant height

The general rule of thumb with regard to heights is perfectly sensible – plant the shorter plants at the front and the taller ones at the back.

Plants with useful sculptural shapes

Acanthus	Inula magnifica
spinosus	Ligularia
Alcea rosea	Macleaya
Angelica	cordata
archangelica	Miscanthus
Cortaderia	sinensis
selloana	Onopordum
Crambe cordifolia	Phormium tenax
Cynara	Rheum
cardunculus	Ricinus
Delphinium	Stipa gigantea
Gunnera	Telekia speciosa
manicata	Verbascum

This can, however, produce a very regimented picture, rather like a school choir, so try to vary this slightly by bringing some taller plants forwards. This will break the formality and also obscure some plants, so that they are revealed only as you walk along the length of the border, making it more interesting.

There are some plants, such as *Verbena bonariensis*, that, while tall, are also very sparse and wiry. Such plants can be planted towards the front of the border, where they will create a misty effect as you look through them to the plants behind.

Working with different shapes

Finding good ways to work with plant shapes is more complex than working with height. Learn by looking at other gardens and deciding what you think works well. Contrasting shapes certainly make a border more interesting. So, the sword-like leaves of an iris contrast well when planted in front of the giant leaves of a *Rheum* (ornamental rhubarb) or the filigree foliage of *Myrrhis* (sweet cicely). Likewise, frothy grasses or the sword-like spikes of an iris work well with the more substantially leaved hostas.

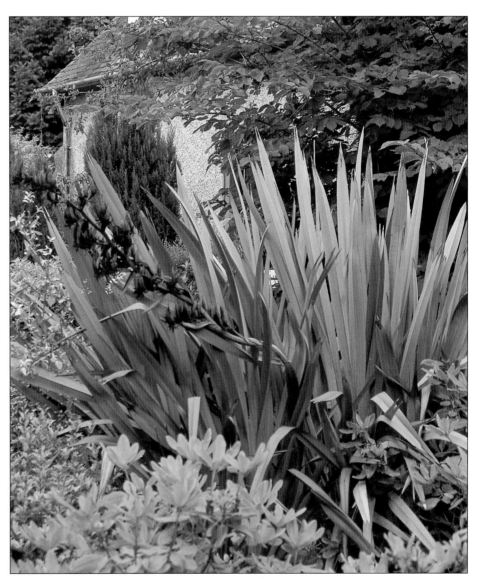

Here, sword-like, spiky leaves draw the eye up and away, and in doing so create a sudden burst of energy in the middle of the border.

Ground-cover plants

Very few gardeners have as much time to spend in their gardens as they would wish, and so anything that helps to save them some time in the garden is well worth considering. Ground cover is one such valuable aid: it cuts down the amount of weeding needed, and covers large areas with just one plant, so saving on planting.

What are ground-cover plants?

They are exactly what the name suggests: plants that cover the ground. Some are creeping plants that spread out to form a dense mat, others are a large planting of individual plants, each one merging into the next to provide a close mass. Most tend to be low-growing, though this is not essential, and any dense-growing plant will suffice. Some gardeners consider any plants grown closely together as ground cover, but the term is usually reserved for those plants that have a proven record for dense growth.

Most ground-cover plants flower at some point, but they are mainly used as foliage plants, which ensures that they cover the ground for the maximum length of time. Many can simply be left until they die back naturally, but others, such as pulmonarias, are best sheared over at the end of flowering so that they acquire a set of fresh and more attractive leaves.

Purposes of ground cover

There are several reasons for using ground cover. The first and most obvious one is that a dense covering of plants inhibits the germination and growth of weeds from beneath them. In other words, it cuts down the amount of weeding that is required for the area they cover.

Another use is to cover large areas with attractive plants. This is particularly important in large gardens, where there are often areas that need planting but are not suitable for borders, such as under trees, where a carpet of plants can be very attractive.

A third use of ground cover is to deal with areas that are difficult to cultivate. Banks, for example, may be awkward to cope with, as are those barren strips of earth in the middle of some driveways, which are the perfect place for thymes or similar low-growing plants.

Limitations of ground cover

Ground cover is not all good news, however. There are some downsides, particularly if you have only a small garden, where space is a premium

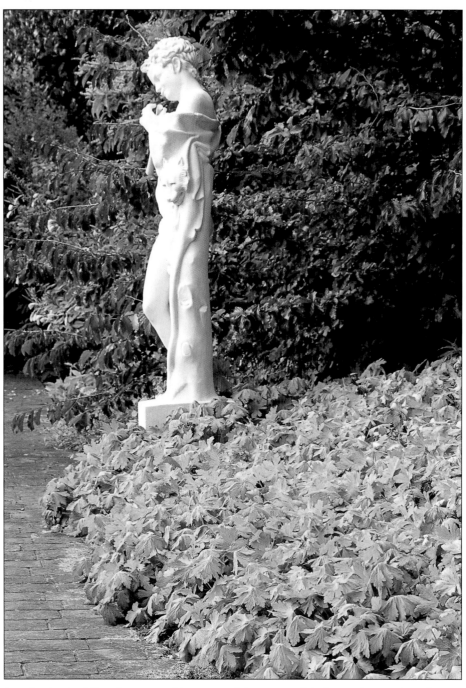

A perfect bank of *Geranium macrorrhizum*, one of the most useful of ground cover plants for creating an effectively impenetrable layer.

Geranium macrorrhizum will grow in dry conditions in fairly dark shade, and yet it not only gives good leaf cover, but also provides attractive flowers.

Use plants such as *Pratia* to carpet and soften paving that is not walked on.

(though for larger gardens the advantages certainly outweigh the disadvantages).

The first is that a large spread of the same plant can be rather boring. This may not trouble you if you are not over-interested in plants as such but just want to keep your garden tidy. However, many gardeners feel that they would rather use their space for different plants, creating a more interesting scene.

The second disadvantage is that ground cover is not quite as efficient as it is often portrayed to be. Any perennial weeds left in the ground when it was prepared will certainly penetrate the cover, and any thinning of the cover will allow in light and aid the germination of weed seed. So it is essential to prepare the soil thoroughly in the first place, removing all traces of weeds, and then to make certain that the plants

are in the best of health and maintain their tight cover. Shearing them over from time to time helps to keep them dense.

The third problem is rubbish. So often ground-cover areas are left to themselves, and they have a habit of catching any pieces of paper or other bits of rubbish that blow past. You just need to remember to check the plants every so often and remove any rubbish that has accumulated.

Ground-cover plants

Acaena	Geranium
Alchemilla mollis	nodusum
Anemone x	Geranium x
hybrida	oxonianum
Bergenia	Gunnera
Brunnera	Hosta
macrophylla	Houtuynia
Convallaria	cordata
majalis	Lysimachia
Crambe cordifolia	nummularia
Epimedium	Maianthemum
Euphorbia	Persicaria affinis
amygdaloides	Petasites
robbiae	Pulmonaria
Geranium x	Rheum
cantabrigiense	Rodgersia
Geranium	Symphytum
endressii	Tiarella cordifolia
Geranium	Tolmiea menziesii
macrorrhizum	Vancouveria

Hostas always provide good ground cover, as long as the soil is not too dry. Use a mix of the different varieties to inject more visual interest.

Climbing plants

Most climbing plants are shrubby, but there are a number of herbaceous perennials and annuals that can be used to great effect as climbers in the garden. They have the advantage over shrubby climbers in that there is no complicated pruning regime: they are simply cut back or removed at the end of the season.

Climbing and scrambling
Most of the herbaceous and annual climbers are really scramblers rather than true climbers. Ivy, for example, will stick to any surface, and honeysuckle will twine its way up anything. In other words, they can scramble up through other plants, using them for support, rather than twining their way up a pole. Nasturtiums, for example, will not climb up a simple tripod or post but will happily scramble up through a bush, to a surprising height.

The few true climbers include the golden hop (*Humulus lupulus* 'Aureus'), which will climb up poles or even a thin string or wire. Sweet peas are another good example: they have tendrils and can cling to their support, but are often helped by being tied in at regular intervals.

Vertical planting
A three-dimensional garden is much more interesting than one on a single level: by adding height you break the monotony of a flat appearance. Height can be achieved by tall plants but further height can be obtained by using climbers held on a variety of poles, trellises or other supports.

Supports
A wide variety of supports can be used. Being mainly scramblers, most herbaceous and annual climbers are best grown through some form of twiggy framework. This could be pea sticks (branches of trees or shrubs such as hazel cut in winter) stuck in the ground. Alternatively, the climbers can be allowed to scramble up through a low-growing shrub, often providing colour after the shrub has finished flowering. Another option is a tripod of poles with string or netting wrapped round it to give the plant support.

For true climbers, such as hops or *Cobaea*, poles, strings, trellises or frameworks can be used. These can also be used by scrambling plants, as long as they are tied to the supports.

Sweet peas are probably the most widely grown of all annual climbers. They work in so many different types and styles of gardening.

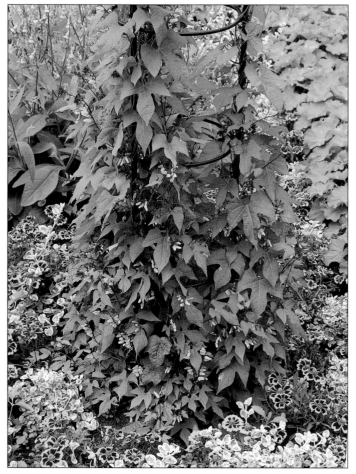

Ipomoea lobata is a valuable annual climber and is one of the few that works well in colourful or exotic bedding schemes.

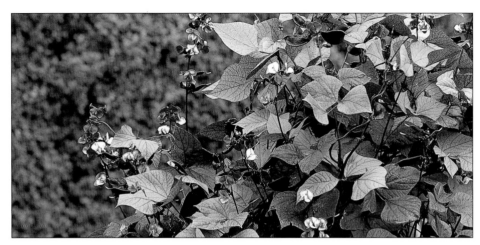

Lablab purpureus has become a very popular annual climber, partly because of its pea-like flowers and seed pods and partly due to its attractive purple foliage.

Marginal planting

While height can be used anywhere you like in the garden, one of the more favoured areas is around the margins. This is partly because this will form a backdrop to the rest of the garden and partly because it can be used to screen out neighbouring gardens or buildings. Trellising provides a good support for this kind of position.

Another way of using climbers around the margins is to use them on walls. Here they may cover an ugly wall or simply be used to break up its expanse. The most likely reason for keen gardeners, however, is that it is simply an available space on which yet another plant can be grown.

Different heights

With the exception of hops, the annual *Caiophera* and one or two others, herbaceous and annual climbers are not very vigorous and will not climb to great heights.

Those that can reach greater heights, however, can be used to climb over a frame to form an arbour or a pergola. Hops, for example, create a wonderfully dappled shade that is perfect for sitting under.

Less energetic climbers can also be used in conjunction with more vigorous shrubby climbers. For example, *Eccremocarpus* will grow to advantage through the bare base of clematis, which often shed their lower leaves.

Extending the season

Growing climbers through shrubs or other plants can add to the length of the flowering season. Most annual and perennial climbers flower from midsummer onwards, as the plants have to put on quite a large amount of growth before they bloom. Many shrubs flower in spring, after which they can be considered a foliage plant, but growing a late-flowering climber through them gives them another lease of life. Virtually all perennial and annual climbers can be used in this way.

Convolvulus tricolor 'Royal Ensign' has long been a popular favourite and is widely grown for its lovely flowers.

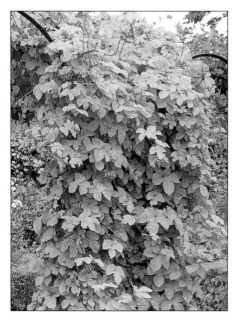

The golden hop, *Humulus lupulus* 'Aureus', is a fast-growing perennial climber that will densely cover a pergola, arbour or framework.

Gardening techniques

Gardening is one of those imprecise sciences in which there are often several ways of achieving the same results – and equally enthusiastic proponents for each different method. For example, one of the most successful commercial propagators achieves incredible results simply by pushing cuttings straight into the compost (soil mix), leaves and all, yet most other gardeners would throw up their hands in horror at this.

Having said that, there are many basic routines and techniques that are universally accepted as working well and which have been proved by constant use over many centuries. Many of these are included in this section. The best approach is to start by following the advice given here, but if you find that certain things work better for you when you use another method, then by all means stick with that. All our garden environments – soils, climates and plantings – are different, as is the temperament of each gardener, so it is not surprising that techniques will vary from garden to garden.

What follows are reliable, widely accepted routines recommended to achieve and maintain an attractive garden – in particular, one filled with annuals and perennials. However, since the techniques are basic ones that apply generally to all kinds of gardening, any beginner following them will get a thorough grounding that will be useful in any garden.

The excellent supports for these delphiniums will soon become invisible, hidden by the plants' foliage.

Soil preparation

Preparing the soil properly is one of the most important tasks that a gardener performs. No matter how well you design your garden, you will not get any decent results unless you have taken some trouble in preparation. This is particularly important where perennial plants are concerned, as these will remain in situ for many years without any chance of having their soil revitalized, except at surface level.

Ideal soils

Short of excavating the whole site and replacing it with perfect soil, you will have to manage with the soil that exists in your garden. However, it is possible, and usually desirable, to modify the soil to make it as near perfect as possible.

The perfect soil is a loamy one, which is open to allow free drainage of excess moisture but contains sufficient organic material to retain enough moisture for the plants. But even this ideal soil may need modifying in certain circumstances.

If you grow woodland plants, for example, then more organic material should be added to keep the soil moist, like the leaf mould that naturally forms under the trees. In addition to improving the condition of the soil, this organic material will also provide a great deal of nutrition for the plants. If, on the other hand, you grow Mediterranean-type plants, then they are likely to need sharper drainage, so more grit should be added to the soil.

Improving the soil

The best way to improve soil is to add well-rotted organic material as you dig it over. Make sure that you maintain the soil's levels of nutrition by top-dressing it with more material over the years.

Well-rotted farmyard manure is still one of the best soil conditioners.

Nowadays there is a really wide range of organic material readily available. Some of this will be sold by your local garden centre, but the very best kind is homemade garden compost (soil mix).

Farmyard manure is another excellent organic choice, but this needs to be well rotted before it can be put on the soil, and you may not always have the space – in a place where you don't mind strong smells lingering – to leave it to rot. Stables are a good source of manure, and it can often be had for free as long as you collect it yourself.

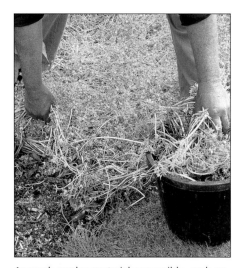

As much garden material as possible, such as these spent annuals, should be composted and returned to the soil.

Leaf mould can be made by collecting fallen leaves and allowing them to rot down. The leaves should be collected from your own garden or road, then either placed in a mesh enclosure or put in bags, punctured at intervals to allow air in. Do not go down to the woods and remove leaves from under the trees, as this will upset the natural balance. Bags of composted bark or other material mixed with farmyard manure are sold by garden centres and nurseries.

Avoid using peat, as this breaks down rapidly in the soil, has little nutritive value and is unsound environmentally, as the peat bogs are fast becoming depleted.

Heavy soils also benefit from having grit added to them. The best size is horticultural grit, which is about 4mm/⅛in in diameter.

Composting

Buy or make a compost (soil mix) bin and fill it with any material you cut from the garden: spent plant stems, leaves and flowers, grass cuttings, shredded hedge and shrub trimmings. Also add any non-cooked vegetable waste from the kitchen, such as peelings.

Avoid adding thick layers of just one material, such as grass cuttings, which can go very slimy. It is better to add thinner layers of different materials in order to keep the compost well balanced, and to fork the heap over now and then. Adding more material is a constant process – continue until the box is full.

Ideally, you should have three boxes: one that you are adding to, one that is rotting down and almost ready to use, and one from which you are using the ready compost. Water the material if it is too dry, and keep each box covered. Leave until it has rotted down into a crumbly, sweet-smelling compost.

MAKING A NEW BED

1 Mark out the bed with a garden line or, as here, with canes. It is very important to remove all perennial weeds. Try to do this by hand if possible. If you do use weedkiller, always apply it according to the maker's instructions on the packet, and make sure you leave the bed until all the weeds have died.

2 Start digging a new bed by making a trench one spade's depth deep across one end. Place the excavated soil into a wheelbarrow and take it to the other end of the plot, where it will be used to fill in the final trench.

3 Now place a layer of well-rotted organic material – such as garden compost (soil mix) or farmyard manure – along the bottom of the trench, breaking it up and spreading it over the soil. Be generous and use as much material as possible.

4 Dig the next row, tipping the soil on top of the compost, filling in the first trench and creating a new one. Add compost to the bottom of this and repeat until the whole plot is dug, leaving the final trench empty.

5 Add a layer of compost to the final trench and then fill it in using the soil excavated from the first trench. The digging is now complete and if time allows, you can leave the bed over the winter so the weather will break the soil down.

6 If prepared in the autumn, by the spring the weather will have broken down the soil to a fine tilth (consistency). Remove any weeds that have reappeared and then rake over the bed, using the back of the rake to break up any larger lumps if necessary.

Clearing the weeds

It is vital to remove any perennial weeds from the planned borders or beds before you start any planting, as you will never be able to clear them once the plants are growing. With lighter soils, this can be done by digging the beds over and removing the weeds by hand. With heavier soils, it may be necessary to use herbicides. If this is done properly, it should be a one-off operation and there will be no need to reapply chemicals, so no damage will be done to the environment.

You can cover the area to be cleared with black plastic or an old carpet to stop weed growth, but this must be left in place for up to two years to be certain that the tougher

Organic materials

Garden compost (soil mix)
Farmyard manure
Leaf mould
Spent mushroom compost
Seaweed
Spent hops
Composted bark

weeds have died off. Unless the bed is out of sight, you may not want to have this unattractive covering on view for such a long time.

Digging the soil

Always aim to dig soil over several months before the bed is to be planted, adding in organic material as you go and removing any weeds. Leave it for three or four months and then remove any weeds that have returned or resprouted. Fork or rake the soil over, and then the bed should be ready for planting.

Acquiring plants

There are various different ways of obtaining plants to stock your garden. The most obvious one is to buy them from some source or another, although this can turn out to be an expensive option. If you are lucky, friends and family may give them to you. You could also grow some plants yourself – from seed, cuttings or divisions.

Plant quality

If you buy your plants, you must always try to obtain the very best. Poor-quality plants may be cheaper, but they will rarely develop in the way you hope they might and so can be a disappointment. The best plants are not necessarily the largest ones, as they often take a while to settle down, allowing more modest plants to overtake them. Those of a medium size are usually best.

The plant should be in character (in other words, growing in the way that nature intended, whether bushy, slender or hummock-forming), and not be drawn or stunted. The new growth should be strong and bushy. Below the soil, the roots should not be pot-bound (wound around and around the pot in a tight mass). This can be checked by simply removing the plant carefully from its pot and having a look.

An interesting garden has a large number of different plants, which can be acquired from a variety of sources.

Another very important thing to check for when obtaining plants is whether the plant is diseased or harbouring any pests. If it looks sick or is covered in greenfly (aphids), you should reject it out of hand. Finally, don't choose a plant in full flower unless you want to be certain of the flower colour; it is better to choose one that is still in bud.

Buying plants

A large number of different outlets sell plants these days, from nurseries and garden centres to your local grocery store or neighbour's yard sale. There are no fixed rules about which is best but there are some useful points to bear in mind.

Many specialist nurseries are extremely good places to stock up, as the owners will grow their own plants, which are frequently of high quality. As well as being knowledgeable, the owners are often sole operators with small overheads, so the plants may be cheaper than those in larger garden centres.

Plants in your local grocery store are often left over from other sales points and may be pot-bound. They are less likely to be looked after properly and may be unlabelled or labelled incorrectly (as can be the case with plants sold at local fairs).

Plants as gifts

This is one of the best ways of obtaining plants. Not only are they free, but, if you have admired a plant, and a cutting is then taken for you or the plant divided, you know exactly what you are getting. It is wise to make a note of a plant's name straightaway, especially if you have been given several different cuttings or divisions.

If you think that a dug-up plant may be infected with root pests, wash off all the soil and pot it up in fresh compost (soil mix). Put any cuttings you are offered straight into a plastic bag and seal it. Pot them up as soon as possible.

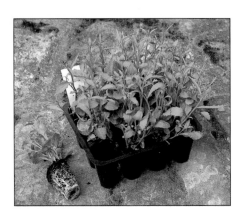

Plants can be obtained as "plugs", which contain only a small amount of compost and need transplanting as soon as possible.

Bigger plants can be obtained in modules or in pots. These also need to be potted on to larger containers or planted out.

Do not buy pot-bound plants (left). The roots should be evenly spread through the compost (soil mix) and not tightly wound (right).

Whole trays of modules can be purchased from garden centres, saving the trouble of raising your own plants.

It is quite easy (and cheaper) to obtain plants by increasing your own stock. Here, cuttings are being taken from home-grown dahlias.

Signs of a healthy plant

General healthy appearance
Strong growth
Not drawn or too big
Not too small or stunted
No pests or diseases
No roots wound around inside the pot or container

Growing your own

In many ways, growing your own plants is the most satisfying way of stocking your garden, as you have the satisfaction of feeling that you have created something from nothing. Seed is still fairly cheap and is widely available in a wonderful range of perennials and annuals. You do not need much equipment to germinate them and grow them on; most can be grown in open soil.

Seeds can be bought from seed companies, garden centres and some general-purpose stores. There are also specialist societies that run seed exchanges, where you can get unusual seeds not carried by other sources. Certain botanical gardens also offer seed that can be difficult to obtain elsewhere, so giving you the chance to grow some unusual and unique plants. You can, of course, collect your own seed and propagate from this. This is not difficult and can be very rewarding, as you are actively involved with every stage of the plant's life.

There are other methods of propagating plants – dividing and taking cutting from your own plants, for example. This does mean that you won't be introducing new plants to your garden, but it is the perfect way of increasing your stock of favourite plants and ideal if you need large numbers of the same plants for creating drifts of colour.

Choosing plants for a low-maintenance garden

The ideal low-maintenance garden uses hard surfaces rather than grass, to reduce or eliminate the need for mowing. If you take this route, choose plants that you think will look good in this kind of situation – you might want more colourful or luxuriant plants to make up for the lack of green lawn, for example. Remember that using ground cover reduces the need for weeding.

Concentrate on plants that are self-supporting, so that you do not need to do any staking. Also, try to use plants that do not need deadheading and only require cutting back once a year. Foliage plants such as hostas are ideal in these kinds of situations. Long-flowering annuals are also a boon, as they will perform for the whole summer with only the occasional bit of attention – just some deadheading and the cutting back of straggling stems.

Containers and hanging baskets need daily watering and deadheading to look at their best, so you may want to stick to plants in beds, which need far less watering. Reduce the need for watering further by using plenty of mulches, which help to prevent water evaporation from the soil and cut down on weeding.

Low-maintenance plants

Acaena
Alchemilla mollis
Antirrhinum
Bergenia
Epimedium
Geranium macrorrhizum
Hosta
Impatiens
Pelargonium
Penstemon
Persicaria affinis
Pulmonaria
Tagetes
Vancouveria

Border plants can be lifted and divided in spring to provide more plants. *Sisyrinchium striatum* (seen here) are easy to divide.

Planting

Take your time when planting new acquisitions. The more attention they are given, the better they will establish themselves and the better they will continue growing. After all, there is no point in buying or raising plants from seed only to kill them later on. The techniques are simple and mainly common sense, but they are worth emphasizing.

Vital preliminaries

The importance of good soil preparation has already been explained, but it is worth restating that soil must be properly prepared prior to any planting. Even if you are just filling a gap in a bed or border, it is still worth digging over the spot, removing any weeds and adding well-rotted garden compost (soil mix) to rejuvenate it. An hour or so before planting, give the plants, still in their pots, a thorough watering.

If the weather is wet or the soil very wet, avoid planting until it has dried out or you will compact the soil. If it is necessary to get on with the planting, use a plank of wood to walk on to spread your weight.

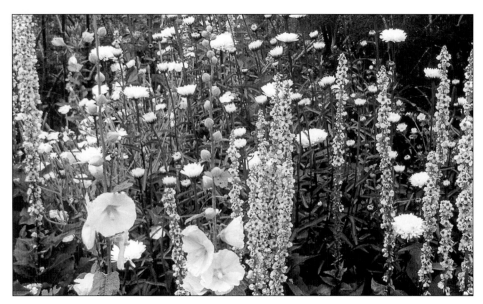

This attractive border, featuring yellow and gold perennials, has benefited greatly from thorough soil preparation before any planting was done.

Finding the right place

There are two considerations to make when deciding where to plant: one visual and the other physical. Whether you are planting up a whole border or just filling a small gap, it is important to try to visualize what the small plant you have in your hand will look like when it is fully grown.

You will have to consider how big your plant will eventually become and how it will relate to its neighbours. Is it far enough away from them to avoid swamping them? Is it short enough not to hide the plants behind it or tall enough to be seen over the plants in front? Is it the right colour and shape for this spot? All these things must be considered before you start to plant. It is especially important to get it right the first time with perennials, if you can, as you may not want to move them for several years.

Plenty of space has been left around the various plants in this gravel bed. This allows them to develop healthily without swamping each other.

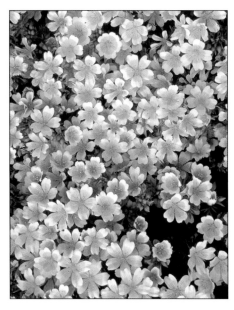

Limnanthes douglasii is an excellent annual for filling in temporary gaps in a perennial border.

PLANTING A BED

1 If the bed was dug in the autumn, winter weather should have broken down the soil. In spring, rake over the soil and remove weeds. Sprinkle bonemeal over the top of the soil to give plants a good start (wear rubber or latex gloves when handling bonemeal preparations).

2 Draw a grid on a planting plan and then mark out a scaled-up version on the bed, using sand or compost (soil mix). Alternatively, you can use string stretched between canes to mark out the planting plan.

3 Using your planting plan and grid as a guide, lay out the plants, still in their pots, on the ground. Now stand back, and try to envisage the border as it will be, and make any necessary adjustments.

4 Dig a hole with a trowel or spade and, with the plant still in its pot, check that the depth and width is right. Adjust if necessary.

5 Remove the plant from the pot and place in the planting hole. Fill in the hole with soil and then firm the plant in.

6 When the bed is completely planted, water in all the plants. They should be kept watered until they have become established.

Temporary fillings

Perennial plants will usually take a while, sometimes up to several years, to fill out their allotted space properly. Rather than have bare earth showing while you are waiting, it is an excellent idea to fill the space with annuals. Temporary gaps in a border can also be filled with annuals. It's not a good idea to choose young annuals for this job, as they will take time to develop. Instead, keep back a few annuals growing in pots, so that they can be used as mature plants, ready to fill any space immediately.

7 Cover the soil between the plants with a layer of mulch, such as composted bark, to keep weeds down and preserve moisture.

8 If you are concerned that you will not remember what the plants are, mark each one with a plastic label. If you always put these labels in the same place – say, to the right of the plant – you can hide them from view and yet still locate them if necessary at any time.

Staking

Supporting plants is one of those tasks that many of us never seem to get around to until it is too late and the plants have collapsed in a messy heap. At this stage, trying to give them some form of support always spells disaster, as the plants look as though they have been forced into a straitjacket. The answer is to get the stakes into place before they are actually needed.

Why stake?

Some plants are used to growing in isolation and have strong stems that need no support, while others are more used to growing closely with other plants, giving each other mutual support. In the garden, an artificial situation is created and plants are often grown in discrete clumps, often with bare earth between them, which leaves them vulnerable to winds.

Plants with especially large or double flower heads are good candidates for staking. The heavy heads often make the plant droop over, particularly after rain, when the sheer number of petals means that the flower holds a lot of rainwater.

One way to avoid staking is to choose short cultivars such as this dahlia, 'Bishop of Llandaff', which needs no support.

To keep your garden looking at its best, always support the heavier and taller plants. Even low-growers may flop and need support, especially those next to a path or lawn.

Alternatives to staking

One way to keep everything upright without stakes is to emulate nature and place your plants close together, so that they support one another. This does, however, inevitably affect the appearance of the border, and so is perhaps best suited to informal and cottage-style gardens. Another natural way of offering support is to

Proprietary stakes can be used to form a linked hoop around and through the plant. They are available in different heights.

allow sprawling plants, such as geraniums, to clamber up through the lower branches of shrubs.

Timing

The most important thing about staking is not to wait until the plant is fully grown but to apply supports when the plant is about a third to half grown. In this way the stems of the plant will grow up through the support, and a few will emerge outside the framework, therefore hiding it in a very natural way. The hidden stakes will then make a good job of supporting the plant.

Hoops with cross wires make excellent supports but are rather inflexible as their width cannot be adjusted.

A hoop on a single pole can have its height adjusted as an individual plant grows, so giving it continual support.

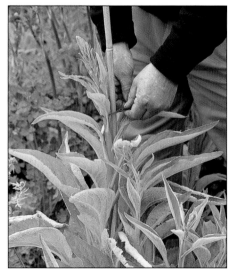

A tall, single-stemmed plant can be supported with a cane (stake). Place it at the back of the plant, where it cannot be seen.

A network of pea sticks (branches or twigs from a shrub) can be erected over or around a plant clump to support plants as they grow.

Individual stems

Some plants, such as foxgloves, have one main flowering stem, and if these are weak or in a particularly exposed position, then they may need support. In this type of situation, a single cane (stake) – preferably painted green – can be inserted into the soil immediately behind the plant, so that it is hidden from view as much as possible. Tie the plant stem to the cane with soft string. Another alternative here is to use the widely available proprietary supports that feature an upright rod and a holding ring.

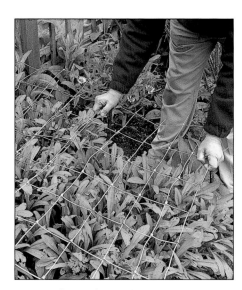

A sheet of stock fencing held horizontally on posts will give secure support to a plant covering a large area.

STAKING LILIES

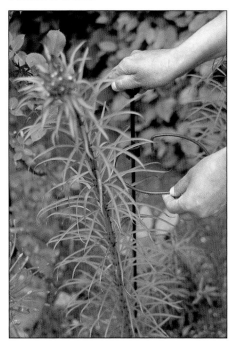

1 First position the metal stake, about 15cm (6in) away from the emerging stem. Now release one side of the ring and carefully trap the lily stem within.

Home-made supports

Pea sticks (usually branches of shrubs such as hazel, cut in the winter) make good supports. Push them into the ground around the clump, then bend the tops over and intertwine them to form a horizontal mesh just above the growing plant. Tie the twigs together for extra support. If twigs are not available, stick in a number of canes around the plant and weave a web of strings between them, again forming a mesh through which the plant will grow.

For a large clump of plants, place several stout sticks around and in the clump, and tie a piece of large-mesh wire netting to them so that it is supported horizontally just above the growing plant. The stems will then pass through this as they grow.

Proprietary supports

All kinds of ready-made supports are currently available, from a range of outlets. Some of these are hoops

2 Clip the second end of the ring into the hole that is provided on the metal support. The lily now has freedom to move but is not able to stray too far.

supported horizontally above the plant, while others consist of individual stakes linked together around and across the plant. Although these are relatively expensive, they do a good job, are easily assembled and taken down, and will last for a very long time.

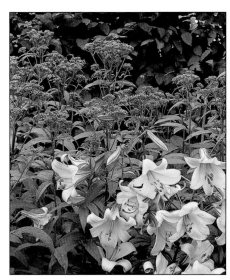

Staking should give plants the support they need, but must be well hidden so that the plants' beauty is not spoiled.

Watering and feeding

Plants, like animals, will not grow without water and food. To a certain extent, these are naturally provided for by way of rainfall and nutrients available from the atmosphere and from decaying vegetation. The competition for water and nutrients in a crowded border, however, frequently means that there is not enough natural supply in a full garden. These supplies can also partially or completely fail. This is why it is important keep a garden well watered and fed.

A good soaking

The principal thing about watering is that you should always make certain that adequate water is applied. Watering so that only the surface of the soil is damp will make the plant's roots grow towards the surface rather than deep down, which leaves the plant vulnerable during hot periods or times when you do not water. As a rule of thumb, try to give the equivalent of 2.5cm/1in of rain each time, which should ensure that the ground around the plant or the compost (soil mix) in the container is soaked.

Methods of watering

Watering cans are easy and versatile to use, and enable you to put the water exactly where you want it.

A well-watered and fed border will keep the plants looking fresh and lasting longer.

However, they do make the job quite arduous if you have a lot to do. Special pump-action watering cans can be used to water containers that are above head height, such as hanging baskets.

You can fill your watering cans from water butts placed under any drainpipes from roofs to collect rainwater. This means that not only are you "recycling" rainwater in the same way that nature would do, but also that you are watering your garden with water that is not full of chemicals and is also, for those on water meters, free.

For larger areas, garden hoses are useful. These can be connected to sprinklers, which deliver water in droplet form, like rain. To give you a rough idea of how long it takes to deliver the necessary 2.5cm/1in, place a jam jar or similar container somewhere under the sprinkler. Hand-held sprays can also be attached to hoses, but again you must be sure to apply enough water before moving on to the next plant.

Another way is to use a dribble system, whereby a special hose with small holes in it is laid throughout the border, so that water slowly

Plants can be watered individually by using a lance spray attached to a hose. This is time-consuming but worth the effort.

A large area can be covered with a sprinkler. Place jam jars or other containers around the area to judge the amount of water delivered.

A dribble hose (a hose with holes in it) can be hidden among plants in a border to allow gentle, controlled watering.

Mulching will help to preserve the moisture in a border by cutting down the amount of water that evaporates.

It is possible to feed as you water, using special attachments that add a controlled amount of fertilizer to the water.

Granular or pelleted fertilizer can be scattered around the plant, ensuring that it is only used where it is needed.

dribbles out over a long period of time. These pipes can be buried below the mulch, thus reducing wastage through evaporation.

Watering with hoses or sprinklers may be subject to local water authority controls, especially during drought conditions, when you will need them most. There may also be regulations regarding connections to the water mains. Check that you are not infringing any regulations.

Preserving moisture

In addition to watering, it is important to preserve as much of the moisture in the soil as you can for plant use. The best way to do this is to cover the soil with a mulch, such as leaf mould, grass cuttings or composted or chipped bark. A layer of about 10cm/4in is ideal. Apply the mulch either after rain or after watering the bed thoroughly.

Feeding

In the garden, we tend to clear the beds of all dying and dead vegetation, so there is little chance of it rotting down where it lies and returning to the soil as nutrients, as would happen in the wild. However, the prudent gardener does not throw away all these leftovers but composts them and then returns them to the soil, which considerably increases the nutritional value of the soil.

Preparing the soil thoroughly with garden compost will pay great dividends, but the added nutrients will not last forever. In the case of annuals, the soil can be prepared afresh each year, but for perennials, which are left in situ for several years, it is impossible to do this. It is, however, possible to top-dress the soil each autumn or spring by covering the soil with a mulch of well-rotted garden compost, farmyard manure or composted bark. This can be worked into the top

layer of the soil with a fork, while being careful not to disturb the plants' roots. Alternatively, it can be left on the top as a mulch, which the worms will gradually take down below the surface. The nutrients it contains will in any event be washed down towards the roots by the rain.

If a mulch is not available, a balanced fertilizer can be used instead to add nutrients, spread at the manufacturer's recommended levels, but this is second-best to organic material.

Collecting your own water

Place a water butt underneath the gutter of a greenhouse, shed or garage to catch the water as it runs off the roof. Rainwater is slightly acidic and so is ideal for watering acid-loving plants, especially if you live in a hard-water area. It will also save water and money spent on metered water.

You can easily collect sufficient water in a water butt to keep a collection of acid-loving plants perfectly happy right through the summer. If you are more ambitious, you can now obtain kits that link water butts together, so creating a really effective water storage system for your garden.

The butt should be easy to use, so make sure there is room to get a water can under the tap. Keep the butt covered at all times so that the water remains sweet and clean.

You can also recycle water that has been used for washing or bathing in the house. Known as "grey-water", it is suitable for applying to established plants in borders and on lawns, but is best used immediately and not stored.

Weeding

This is the aspect of gardening that the majority of people dislike the most. However, this is usually because they leave it much too late and by the time they do make the time for it, the beds are infested with weeds and it becomes an uphill battle to clear them. When weeding is done on a regular basis, it can be very quick and even pleasurable, and the resulting weed-free beds are always a joy to see.

Timing

As a general rule, the best time to weed is as soon as you see one. If you keep on top of the weeds, weeding rarely becomes a problem and certainly never a chore.

Ideally, you should go over all the beds during the winter or early spring to clear out any weeds. Once cleared of weeds, they should be mulched. If these two processes are done at the beginning of the growing season, then there is a very good chance that you will have little to do later on except pull out the odd rogue that appears. If, however, you wait until the weather warms up before tackling the weeds, you will find that they are ahead of you.

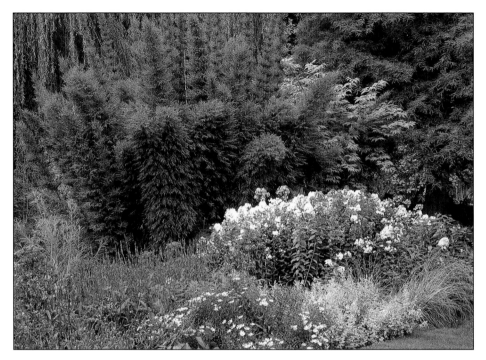

Closely packed planting in a garden border acts as a kind of natural ground cover, usefully suppressing the growth of any weed seedlings.

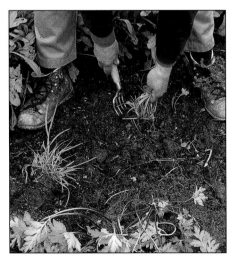

The safest way of controlling weeds in a border is to remove them by hand, rather than with chemicals.

Weed killers

Using chemicals in a planted border is not a good idea. They can be used to make an initial clearance, but once the plants are in place it can be a disastrous procedure. However careful you are, there is bound to be some drift, with odd drops falling on actual plants. Chemicals can also translocate from roots to roots. If a border is prepared properly in the first place and then weeded regularly by hand, there should be no need to use chemicals anyway.

Hand-weeding

The best way to tackle weeds in a border is to hand-weed. If the soil is loose or there is a good depth of mulch on it, this may simply mean pulling the weed gently out. If, however, there is a possibility of the weed breaking off and leaving its roots in the soil, use a hand fork or trowel to loosen the soil first.

In the late winter, as the plants are just appearing through the soil, it is a good idea to fork the soil over lightly, working in well-rotted organic material as you go. As you do this, you can easily pull out any weeds that are present.

If a plant becomes infested with a persistent perennial weed, such as couch grass, then it is best to dig the whole plant out, wash the soil off the roots, remove the weed and replant the plant. If you try to remove the couch grass while the plant is still in the ground, then the pieces of weed that grow through it will only regenerate and you will have to start again.

Hoeing

Some gardeners like to use a hoe to weed their beds, but this can be as dangerous as chemicals. So often, fragile new shoots or even whole plants get hoed off a fraction of a second before you realize that they are not a weed, leading to many lost plants and a considerable amount of bad temper. The other problem is that, although hoeing can be effective for annual weeds, it is no

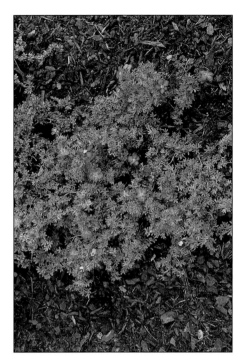

A composted bark mulch will suppress weed growth, but clean the ground well beforehand.

good just cutting off the top of perennial weeds – you need to get the roots out as well.

Mulching

One of the greatest aids to weeding is mulching, since it prevents the weeds from forming in the first

Mulches

Cardboard: effective but ugly
Chipped/composted bark: very good
Farmyard manure: good if weed-free
Garden compost (soil mix): good
Geotextiles and black plastic: good but very ugly
Grass cuttings: good but ugly
Gravel: good in certain areas
Leaf mould: very good
Newspaper: good but very ugly
Peat: poor
Sawdust: good but ugly
Shredded prunings: very good
Spent hops: good
Spent mushroom compost: good
Straw: good but ugly
Woodchips: good but some people find them ugly

place. A layer of some material that will keep the light from the soil will inhibit the germination of weed seeds, so keeping the border free of weeds. If, however, there are already perennial weeds in the border, then the mulch will not help. This is because the weeds will simply grow through the material in the same way as the plants.

Organic mulches, such as leaf mould and composted or chipped bark, are best, as they will eventually rot down and improve the soil. Most

will also look more sympathetic in the borders, creating a good background against which to see the plants, though this is not the case with straw or grass cuttings.

Black plastic mulches are efficient but ugly. Some gardeners try to avoid the plastic showing by covering it with a shallow layer of earth or another mulch, such as bark, but this inevitably washes off in places or is revealed by birds pecking among the covering layer, and the ugly plastic makes a reappearance.

EFFECTIVE WEEDING

1 Where plants are growing close together, the best way of removing weeds is to either pull them out by hand or dig them out using a hand fork. Perennial weeds must be dug out whole and not simply chopped off, or they will soon return.

2 Where there is more room, hoes can be used in a border, but take care not to damage your precious plants in the process. In hot weather, hoed-up weeds can be left to shrivel, but it looks much less messy if they are all removed to the compost heap.

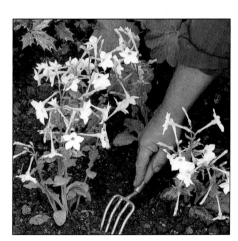

3 After weeding, rake through the border with a fork, or if the plants are far enough apart, with a rake. This will tidy up the bed and level off the surface, removing any footprints and any weed remnants.

4 It is a good idea to apply or renew a mulch after weeding. As well as helping to prevent weeds from reappearing, this will also preserve moisture. Composted or chipped bark will set the plants off well.

Routine plant maintenance

One of the easiest ways of making a garden unattractive is to leave old flower heads and dying stalks on the plants. Trimming them off not only makes the garden look tidier and more appealing but also allows the remaining flowers to shine out and be seen, as well as encouraging new blooms. The three main techniques that will keep your plants both beautiful and healthy are pinching out, deadheading and cutting back.

Getting into the routine

The difference between a garden that is regularly attended and one that is only occasionally looked after is quite amazing, especially towards the end of summer or in the autumn. The dead or dying material not only looks untidy but also obscures those plants that are still fresh. At the start of the season, some judicious pinching out will benefit some annuals from the very beginning.

As with weeding, if you leave deadheading and cutting back for too long, they can become onerous tasks. If you do a little each week, then they become much easier as well as benefiting the appearance of the garden. This applies not only to beds and borders but also to hanging baskets and containers.

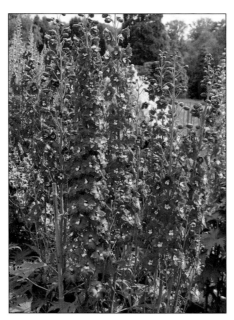

A second flush of delphinium flowers can often be obtained by removing the initial flower spikes as they fade.

Pinching out

If left to their own devices, many plants will grow only one main stem. In a bedding scheme, for example, this would result in a forest of tall spindly spikes with large gaps in between them rather than a desirable carpet of flowers and foliage. To avoid this effect, pinch out the growing tip of each main spike. This will cause the stem to produce side shoots. These will make the plants much more bushy, and further pinching out will increase the effect.

Deadheading

Once a flower starts to fade, you should cut it off. The actual point of the cut varies depending on the plant. If the flower is the only one on the stem, then the whole stem should be cut back to its base. If it is a multi-flowered stem, then the cut should be where the individual flower's stem joins the other stems. If it is a flower spike, then the whole spike should be removed. Try not to leave odd bits of stem sticking up, which looks untidy.

If the foliage is still attractive and the stem is covered with leaves, remove the flower head at some point towards the top of the stem, making the cut close to or behind a leaf so that it does not show. If this is done with, for example, spikes of lupins or delphiniums, you are likely to encourage side shoots, which will produce new spikes of flowers.

Some plants, particularly those with smaller blooms, have masses of flowers, making it almost impossible to deadhead the flowers singly. Geraniums are a good example of this, and the finished flowers are best dealt with as a whole. This means waiting until the majority of the flowers are finished, then cutting over the whole plant or cutting it down completely.

Advantages of deadheading

The improved appearance of plants after deadheading has already been stressed, but there is another benefit to this task too.

If you remove a dying flower, then instead of putting an extraordinary amount of its energy into producing a seed-head, the plant will divert its energy into producing more flowers. So the more you deadhead, the more flowers you are likely to get and the longer the plant will go on flowering.

Removing fading flowers and seed pods from annuals will preserve energy and help to keep them flowering for longer.

Pinching out the main stems from certain annuals and perennials will help them to bush out and develop into a fuller plant.

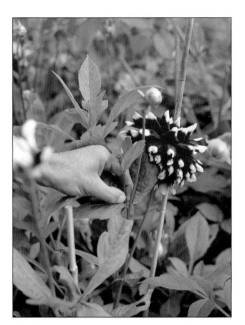

Pinching out the subsidiary shoots of plants such as these dahlias concentrates the growth in the main blooms.

Cutting back

Once early-flowering plants are cut down to the ground, they will re-shoot. In most cases, this means that they will produce a fresh set of leaves, giving the plant a second life as a foliage plant for the rest of the season. Pulmonaria, for example, finish flowering in spring and, if left to their own devices, the leaves will soon become rather tatty and tired-looking. If, however, they are sheared over immediately after flowering, they produce new foliage that remains fresh-looking throughout the rest of the summer. A similar thing happens with *Alchemilla mollis* and many other plants. Some cut-back plants will also have a second flowering.

Once plants are dead or obviously dying, they should be cut back right down to the ground. If plants are cut back so that stumps are left, it becomes difficult to cut next year's stems close to the ground, and so with each year that passes, the plant becomes increasingly surrounded by more, and higher, stumps.

DEADHEADING

1 Using scissors, a sharp knife or secateurs (pruners), snip off the flowers neatly and cleanly where they join the stem. Sometimes the whole head of flowers needs to be removed – cut these back to the first set of leaves. Dead flower heads and other clippings can be added to the compost heap.

On some plants, it is only the taller flowering stems that wilt, while the base of the plant remains green. In such cases, cut off the wilting stems only, as low as possible.

Sometimes, as mentioned above, a plant may still be green but will look rather bedraggled. Here the benefit of being cut down is that it will grow afresh. Such plants should be cut close to the ground, removing all the old growth but leaving any new foliage that might already be

CUTTING BACK GREEN PLANTS

1 Some herbaceous plants remain green throughout winter. Cut back to sound growth, removing dead and leggy material.

2 Regular – and carefully executed – deadheading produces a considerably cleaner and healthier looking arrangement. Dead flowers ruin the best of plants, as well as using up vital energy in seed production. It takes only a short time and the effort is always worthwhile.

appearing among the old stems. In this scenario, cutting back is mainly considered worth the effort for the new growth that appears, as this rejuvenates the plant. Sometimes, however, such new growth is required for propagation purposes. For example, there is not much suitable cutting growth when violas are in full flower or once they have finished flowering, but if they are cut to the ground the new shoots are just perfect for such a purpose.

2 Here, the old stems have been cut off so that they are level with the emerging growth, so as not to damage it.

Autumn and winter tasks

Many non-gardeners think of the cooler months as the dead season, when little is happening. In fact, there is plenty to do: lifting certain plants, removing any remaining dead material, forking over beds to weed them and open the soil, and then top-dressing them. Your garden machinery should also be thoroughly checked over and oiled. Finally, there is the excitement of sitting down with seed catalogues and planning how your garden will look in the coming seasons.

Borders and beds

One thing to make sure you get done before the frosts set in is to lift more vulnerable plants. Tender plants such as pelargoniums should be potted up and overwintered in a greenhouse (or take cuttings if you don't have much storage space). Tender bulbs such as gladioli should be lifted if you live in a cold area, especially if your soil is heavy. Dry them, then store them somewhere frost-free and check every few weeks.

Another major job is to remove all the dead stems and foliage from the previous year. Some gardeners like to leave these as long as possible to provide the birds with a source of food in the form of seeds and any

Winter is a good time for catching up on tool and machinery maintenance. It will save a lot of time when you are busy in spring.

insects that hide in the dead foliage. Others leave it because it gives structure and something to look at during the winter months.

Other gardeners are eager to clear the ground as soon as possible. In addition to giving you a much tidier-looking garden, the main benefit of this is that you avoid leaving the clearing up to the last minute in early spring, when there are suddenly lots of other jobs to do. If work is then delayed due to bad weather, it can have a knock-on effect for the rest of the year.

You can have the best of both worlds if you cut the dead material and then hang it up so that the birds can still get at it. All the material removed from the beds should eventually be composted so that its

goodness can be returned to the soil. Hardened stems are best shredded first, if possible.

Once the borders have been cleared, lightly fork them over to open up the soil and to remove all weeds, before top-dressing them with well-rotted organic material up to 10cm/4in thick. The beds are now well prepared for the next season. Any new planting should be done in either the early autumn or spring.

Avoid working on the beds if the soil is too wet. If it becomes a necessity, then use a wooden plank to stand on, as this will spread your weight and limit damage to the soil.

Winter plant care

Remember that not all plants die back in winter and that there are a surprising number that still produce flowers and foliage. There is generally not much to do to these except enjoy them.

One thing that is generally not required is watering. If, however, you have containers that are in the lee of the house or a wall, so that they get little rain, they should be watered occasionally if the soil gets dry. This should be sparingly done so that the soil is left just moist and not wringing wet.

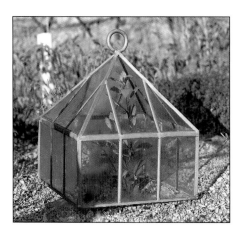

Here is a decorative way of giving slightly tender plants winter protection. Remove the container during warmer, damp weather.

Tender plants such as these pelargoniums need protection in a frost-free glass house during the winter months.

Winter-flowering perennials

Anemone nemorosa
Eranthis hyemalis
Euphorbia rigida
Helleborus:
   H. niger
   H. orientalis
   H. purpurascens
Iris unguicularis
Primula vulgaris
Pulmonaria rubra
Viola odorata

Garden machinery

Once autumn draws in and winter begins, the lawnmowers, strimmers and hedge cutters tend to be put away and forgotten about until they are next needed. This is, however, the ideal time to have them checked over properly and maintained, ready to use next season. Even if you are not doing this straight away, all your machines should be thoroughly cleaned and oiled.

Catalogue joys

One of the most enjoyable aspects of gardening is the planning. The weather may be unsuitable for gardening itself, but there is nothing more pleasurable than sitting down with a pile of catalogues, dreaming of what you could do if only your garden was twenty times larger.

On a more practical note, this is the time to look seriously at the catalogues to choose the seeds and plants you will be using next year in your hanging baskets and borders. The perennial plants may be constant factors, but you have much greater freedom with annuals, and if you are bold enough you can try something completely different. You might be seduced by the novelties in the catalogue or you might decide to change the colour scheme from, say, reds and yellows to blues and yellows, or even to all white.

LIFTING AND REPLANTING DAHLIAS

1 The time to lift the dahlias for winter storage is just as the first frosts blacken the foliage or when it naturally begins to die back. Remove the foliage and cut back the stems, leaving about 20cm (8in) of each one attached to the tuber.

2 Fork gently around the plant, leaving a radius of 25–40cm (10–16in) from the main stem, depending on the amount of growth it has made. Gently lift the root, taking great care not to damage the tubers. Now carefully remove the soil from around the tubers. Heavy soils may need to be washed off with water from a hose or tap.

3 Place the plant upside down in a box so that any moisture can drain from the hollow stems. Store in a dry, frost-free place and remove the soil from the tubers once it has dried off. Dust any damaged tubers with a fungicide such as yellow or green sulphate of ammonia and then place in boxes of barely moist peat. Overwinter in a dry, well-ventilated, cool, frost-free place.

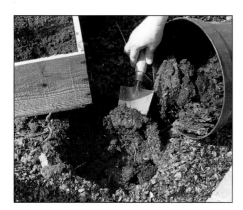

4 When green shoots emerge in spring, water sparingly to keep the compost (soil mix) moist. In late spring or early summer, after all risk of frost has passed, choose a sunny, sheltered spot and prepare a deep planting hole. Add a generous quantity of well-rotted manure or a long-term granular feed, and mix well into the soil at the bottom of the hole.

5 Carefully lower the dahlia into the prepared hole. Add more soil or compost around the plant as necessary to bring up to soil level. The hole should be bigger than the dahlia so that there is room to spread out the tubers. Adjust the hole depth if necessary so that the soil level is the same as the previous year (this level can be seen on the plant).

6 Gently firm the soil surrounding the plant, making sure as you do so that there are no gaps or air-pockets – either around the plant or between the tubers. Firm the soil down first with your hands, gently and carefully, and then more decisively with your foot. Water the plant and the area around it and then add a layer of mulch.

Sowing seeds in pots

There is something immensely satisfying about putting a seed, which is often no larger than a speck of dust, in the ground, knowing that it will eventually grow into a gorgeous plant. This is the basic miracle of nature, and yet although you may plant hundreds of seeds each year, every tiny seedling still seems just as wonderful as the last.

Getting the quantity right

One of the main mistakes made by beginners is to sow too much seed. Unless you are creating a large bedding scheme, you rarely need more than a dozen plants and often,

in the case of perennials, only three or five (odd numbers always look better than even ones in the garden).

Of course, you should grow a few more than you need in case some die, and you may want extras for giving away. If you grow many more than you need, however, you will waste a lot of time pricking the plants out as well as the expense of extra pots and potting compost (soil mix), most of which will end up on the compost heap. For most purposes, you need sow no more than what a 9cm (3½in) pot will contain, and very rarely indeed will you need a half tray, let alone a whole tray.

Sowing your own seed gives you plenty of plants with which you can plan magnificent container or border displays.

A good start

Apart from ending up with too many plants, there are other good reasons for sowing a few seeds at a time in small pots and then pricking out to other pots or trays — and avoiding the temptation to simply sow in trays and then weed the seedlings out. Starting a few seeds at a time gives them the best conditions at the fragile start of their life. You do not want hundreds of germinating seeds vying for goodness from the growing medium, nor do you want intertwined roots. A few good seedlings is preferable to lots of sickly ones, so it is best to transfer to other pots or trays when selecting your strongest seedlings. Also, if space is at a premium, large trays can be a problem.

Composts

For sowing, use a proprietary seed compost (growing medium). This has only a limited amount of fertilizer in it because, at this stage, most of the nutrients will come from the seeds themselves. Once you prick the seedlings out, they will need extra food, and so a potting compost should be used.

SOWING IN POTS

1 Fill the pot to the rim with compost (soil mix) and then gently firm it down. (Don't ram it down, or it will compact.)

2 Sow the seeds thinly across the surface. In the case of large seeds, such as sunflowers, each seed can be placed individually so that they are equidistantly spaced.

3 Cover the seeds, preferably with a layer of horticultural grit, but alternatively with a thin layer of fine compost if grit isn't available. At this stage, remember to label the pot, as one pot of seeds looks very much like another, and you will soon forget which is which.

4 Water the pot either from below, by standing it in a tray of water until the surface of the compost changes colour, or from above, by using a fine-rosed watering can. Place the pot in a propagator or in a shady place in a greenhouse.

There are arguments for and against using either a soil-based compost or a soilless compost as a growing medium, but in the end it comes down to personal preference and what is available locally.

Pricking out

When your seedlings do start to grow, they should be pricked out as soon as their first true leaves make an appearance (this is the second pair of leaves; the first pair are the seed leaves). To prick out your seedlings, place each one very carefully in its own individual pot. Bedding plants, which are often needed in much larger numbers than other plants, are often pricked into trays or cellular trays. The tray is filled with compost and a hole is made for each seedling. Remember that you should never leave plants in trays for too long as they are shallow and the roots will soon become terribly intertwined.

Hardening off

This is a vital part of the process. It is important that you not take plants directly from the greenhouse or cold frame and put them in the garden. The shock of sudden exposure to colder, dryer air could set back their growth significantly or even kill them off completely. Instead, harden the plants off gradually.

A couple of weeks before the plants are needed, place the pots outside for an hour or so each day and then return them to the greenhouse or cold frame. Repeat this process every day, leaving them outside for longer and longer periods of time on each occasion, until eventually they are left out over night. They are now safe to plant out in your garden. If they are tender plants, do not start hardening them off until the threat of frost has passed.

PRICKING OUT INTO POTS

1 If the seedlings have been in a heated propagator, harden them off to the greenhouse temperature before pricking out, by gradually opening the propagator vents over a couple of days. Gently knock out the pot of seedlings on to the bench.

2 Now, proceeding very gently and carefully so that you don't damage the fragile seedlings, break open the ball of compost so that individual seedlings can be removed. The compost should be relatively soft and so this should be fairly easy.

3 Separate the seedlings one at a time as each is required. Always lift and carry a seedling by its leaves, and never by its roots or stem. Use a label or pencil to ease the seedling from the compost without risk of tearing the roots.

4 Hold the seedling over the centre of the pot, keeping your hand steady by resting it against the side of the pot, and pour good quality potting compost around it until the pot is full to the brim.

5 Tap the pot on the bench to settle the compost and then gently firm down with your thumbs or fingers so that the final level is below the rim of the pot.

6 Water the pots with a watering can fitted with a fine rose. Keep the seedlings in the greenhouse or somewhere warm until they have started growing away, then harden them off over a week or more by allowing them increasing amounts of time in the open air, or with a cold frame, by gradually opening it.

Sowing seeds in open ground

Many new gardeners think that all flowers start as seeds grown in pots, but in fact a large number of flowering plants can be sown directly into the soil. This is, of course, what happens in nature anyway. The advantage of pots is that they reduce the competition for food and water, giving the seedlings a flying start. However, if weeds are kept at bay, then the same is true of seeds sown in open ground.

Which seeds to sow outside

You can try sowing virtually any seeds directly into the soil, but there are normally some types that will grow better if they are sown in pots. For example, many annuals, particularly the tender ones, are better started off in pots or trays. This is because you can steal a march on nature by getting them into growth in a greenhouse ready to be planted out as mature plants once the frosts have definitely finished. If you choose to sow them in open ground instead, you would have to wait until the end of the harsh weather, which would then mean that the resulting plants would flower four to six weeks later. In other words, they would not be coming into flower until the summer is almost over.

By contrast, hardy annuals, which will withstand the frosts, can be sown outside in either the autumn or spring, so that the plants are already mature by the beginning of summer. Sowing these plants outside in the first place saves a great deal of time and trouble.

Most perennials can be sown outside, either where they are to flower ultimately or in special beds, but because small numbers are usually involved it is often easier to sow them in pots.

The corncockle, *Agrostemma*, is a plant of disturbed ground that flourishes naturally in cornfields, so it is perfect for sowing in the flower border.

Where to sow

Most directly sown annuals are sown where they are to flower. The exception to this are the biennials, such as wallflowers or sweet Williams, which are usually grown in rows in a seedbed or the vegetable garden and then transplanted into their flowering place in the autumn.

Perennials are normally sown in rows. They can be sown where they are to grow, but because only one, three or five plants are needed at the most, the seedlings can easily get swamped and lost in the hurly-burly of the border. Draw out some shallow drills in the fine soil and sow the seeds thinly along them. Draw some of the soil back over the seeds, then water them. Label each row as you sow it so that you don't forget which is which.

Aftercare

Once your sowing is done, the soil should be kept moist, which may mean watering if the weather is dry. As the seedlings appear, thin them out, making sure that you remove any that are too close together; each plant should have enough room to develop properly. The best rule of thumb here is simple: the larger the final plant, the more space it will

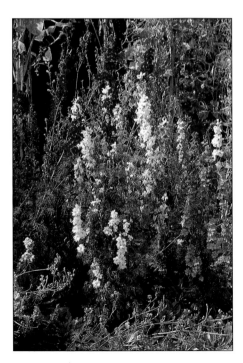

The seeds of different kinds of plants can be scattered over the bare earth to create colourful mixed displays.

SOWING IN OPEN GROUND

1 Thoroughly prepare the ground by digging the soil and breaking it down into a fine tilth (consistency) using a rake. You should not work the soil when it is too wet or it will become compacted.

2 If you plan to use several different blocks of plants, mark out the design on the soil using contrasting coloured sand or compost (soil mix). Broadcast the seed by hand so that it is thinly spread right across the appropriate area. It will probably be necessary to thin out the seedlings when they appear.

3 Gently rake the seed in so that it is covered by a thin layer of soil. Some gardeners prefer to sow their seed in short rows rather than by broadcasting. This makes it easier to weed when the seed first comes up. To sow in rows, first draw out shallow drills with a hoe.

4 Now sow the seed thinly along each row and rake the soil back over them. By carefully thinning the seedlings, the resulting overall pattern of the plants will appear to be random and not in rows.

5 Finally, gently water the whole bed, using a watering can fitted with a fine rose.

6 *(right)* A bed planted with annuals begins to fill out soon after sowing and planting.

require around it. This is not quite so important in row-sown plants as these will be planted into their final positions later. Keep the young plants weeded and healthy.

Transplanting
Plants that are grown in rows elsewhere can be transplanted into their final flowering position as soon as they are large enough to be handled without risk of damaging them. With biennials such as wallflowers, there is no need to do this until the ground has been cleared in the autumn.

With "broadcast" seed (handfuls of seed thrown out over the soil's surface, as opposed to being put into rows of channels), too many plants often develop. Some of these can be dug up carefully and transplanted elsewhere. Water the plants before moving them, and then dig them up, retaining as much soil as you possibly can around the roots. Dig a larger hole than the roots, place the plant in it and then refill with soil, gently but firmly pressing it down, then water again.

Dividing plants

One of the quickest ways of obtaining a new plant is to divide an existing plant into two (or more) pieces and replant both bits. This is not only a method of obtaining new plants but also a way of ensuring that old plants stay young and productive. It is not a difficult technique to learn and soon becomes second nature.

Many hardy geraniums are typical of the type of plant that can be divided to increase their numbers and to keep them healthy.

Double hellebores will only come true if they are increased by division, as seed will often produce inferior plants.

Advantages of dividing plants

Growing new plants from seed is fun and often essential if you want to grow plants to which you would otherwise have no ready access. However, seed can be a bit of a hit and miss method, because you cannot guarantee exactly what you are going to get. A plant is likely to differ from its parent: it may be shorter or taller, the foliage may be slightly different and the colour of the flower can vary considerably.

With annuals, this may not matter or there may be a sufficient degree of conformity, but with perennials it can be more of a problem. It is no good, for example, sowing seed from many of the cultivars of geraniums, as they will not come true. The plants are likely to be inferior (although there is always a chance than one might be better).

Division (and cuttings, which are dealt with elsewhere), by contrast, involves taking a bit of the original plant and reproducing it exactly. This is very important for most named perennial cultivars.

Brute force

There are several ways of dividing a plant. One popular and very easy method is by brute force: simply dig up the plant, cut a chunk off it with a sharp spade and then replant both pieces separately. This is very effective for some of the larger clump-forming plants. It does leave a lot of severed material, which can rot and, in theory, cause problems, but rarely seems to.

A refinement of this is to insert two forks into the dug-up clump, back to back, and then lever them apart, forcing the plant into two pieces, continuing until the pieces are small enough. With the exception of the older, centre pieces of the plant, which should be discarded, the pieces of plant can be replanted immediately. It is, however, always a good idea to use the opportunity to rejuvenate the soil by digging it and adding some well-rotted organic material. The best time to divide plants in this way is the spring.

Manipulation

A more sophisticated approach is to use your hands. Many plants, if shaken so the soil falls off and gently manipulated with the fingers, will fall apart into separate crowns, each of which can be either replanted in the soil or put into pots until they are needed. This is only possible with plants grown in lighter soils, although it is still possible on heavier soils if the plant is manipulated in a bucket of water. More stubborn plants, such as hellebores, can have the water washed off first with a garden hose.

It is difficult to visualize what actually happens until you try it, and then you will be surprised how easily

Using two forks back-to-back is a crude but effective method of division. It is best used with fibrous-rooted plants.

Dividing plants by manipulating them with your hands in a bucket of water produces divisions whose roots are not torn or broken.

the plant comes apart in your hands. Some plants, such as hostas for example, may need a sharp knife to separate the crowns, but generally they just fall apart.

Normally, divisions are made in spring, but if the plants are transferred to pots they can be divided at any point during the growing season.

Replanting

Larger divisions can be treated as normal plants and replanted immediately into the soil. Make certain that the plants are kept moist until they have re-established themselves, and protect them from strong winds. Smaller divisions recover more quickly if they are first grown on in pots and then planted out the following spring. Pot-grown divisions may need hardening off.

Splitting for health

Many perennials get old and woody after a few years. They die off towards the centre of the plant and the flowering becomes less profuse. If these plants are dug up, the old centres thrown away and some of the younger, outside growth replanted, the plant will be totally rejuvenated.

Larger divisions can be planted directly back into the soil – as long as you make sure that they are well watered and mulched.

DIVIDING BY HAND

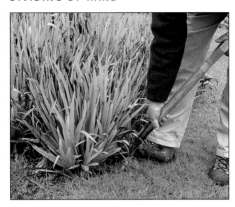

1 Dig up a section of the plant, making sure that it is large enough to provide the quantity of material that you require.

2 Hold the plant firmly at the base and shake it vigorously so that the soil falls off and the roots are exposed.

3 Gently pull the plant into individual pieces, simply by manipulating it with your hands. Many plants, such as this sisyrinchium, will come apart very easily.

4 The pieces should now be potted up individually using a good compost (soil mix). Place in a shaded cold frame for a few days and then harden off.

Plants suitable for division

Acanthus	Epimedium	Lysimachia	Rudbeckia
Achillea	Euphorbia (some)	Lythrum	Salvia (some)
Aconitum	Galega	Meconopsis	Scabiosa
Agapanthus	Geranium (some)	Mentha	Schizostlis
Anaphalis	Helenium	Monarda	Sedum
Anemone	Helianthus	Nepeta	Sidalcea
Anthemis	Helleborus	Ophiopogon	Sisyrinchium
Artemisia	Hemerocallis	Persicaria	Smilacina
Aster	Heuchera	Phlomis	Solidago
Astilbe	Hosta	Phormium	Stachys
Astrantia	Inula	Physostegia	Symphytum
Bergenia	Iris	Polemonium	Tanacetum
Campanula (some)	Kniphofia	Polygonatum	Thalictrum
Convallaria	Lamium	Potentilla	Tradescantia
Coreopsis	Liatris	Primula	Trollius
Crambe	Ligularia	Pulmonaria	Uvularia
Delphinium	Lobelia	Ranunculus	Vancouveria
Epilobium	Lychnis	Rheum	Veronica

Cuttings

Taking cuttings requires slightly more dexterity than dividing plants, but is still surprisingly easy. This is certainly an important technique for a gardener to master, as some plants cannot be reproduced any other way. It is also the ideal method to use when the owner of an admired plant may not want to dig it up and divide it, but is more than willing to snip a little bit off for you.

Why take cuttings?

Like making divisions, taking cuttings is a vegetative way of propagation. In other words, it is taking part of the original plant and reproducing it, and therefore it will have all the same qualities as its parent. It takes a bit more time and trouble than making divisions but is an essential technique as not all plants are easily divided. This is particularly true for those plants that do not spread, but are restricted to a central rosette, as well as many taprooted plants (which have just one long, main root).

Useful equipment

Unlike other propagation methods, you can grow cuttings with various levels of sophistication: equipment varies from costly mist propagators (for the serious gardener who wants

Plants for basal cuttings

Achillea	Lythrum
Anthemis	Macleaya
Artemisia	Mentha
Aster	Monarda
Campanula	Nepeta
Chrysanthemum	Perovskia
Crambe	Phlox
Dahlia	Physostegia
Delphinium	Platycodon
Diascia	Salvia
Epilobium	Scabiosa
Gaillardia	Sedum
Helenium	Senecio (some)
Knautia	Solidago
Lupinus	Verbena
Lychnis	Viola

STRIKING CUTTINGS

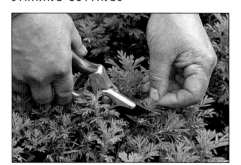

1 Take short cuttings from the new growth at the base of the plant. These cuttings are usually to be found naturally in the spring, but they can be created by cutting the plant hard back so that new growth is formed. Place your cuttings in a plastic bag and then seal the bag.

2 To pot up your cuttings, first trim their base. Cut through the stem just below a leaf joint and then remove all the leaves, except for a few at the top. Make certain that all the cuts are clean and not jagged. A scalpel or sharp scissors are the best tools to use for this purpose, although some gardeners simply use sharp fingernails.

3 Place the cuttings in a pot of cutting compost (planting mix) made up of 50:50 sharp sand and peat or peat substitute. You can grow up to 12 in a pot. If you prefer, dip the bottom 1cm/½in of the cutting in a rooting powder before putting it in the hole. This helps some of the more difficult species to root and also prevents rotting. However, many gardeners find this quite unnecessary for most perennials.

4 Label and date the pot. Thoroughly water and place the pot in a propagator. You can use a plastic bag, but do make sure that no leaves are touching the plastic. Seal with an elastic band.

5 When the roots of the cuttings start to appear at the drainage holes of the pot, gently remove the contents.

6 Pot up the rooted cuttings once again, this time in individual pots, using a good quality potting compost (soil mix). Keep covered for a few days and then harden off.

TAKING ROOT CUTTINGS

1 Very carefully dig the plant out from the ground. You must try to make sure that the thicker roots are not damaged in the process.

2 Now wash away any soil that is clinging to the roots and then remove one or more of the thicker roots.

3 Cut the roots into lengths of about 5–8cm (2–3in). Now make a horizontal cut at the top of the cutting and a slanting cut at the bottom.

4 Fill the pot with a cutting compost (planting mix) and insert the cuttings vertically with the horizontal cut at the top, so that the latter cuts are just level with the soil surface.

5 Cover with fine grit, water and put in a frame. In spring, shoots should emerge and new roots should form. Once you are sure that there are roots, pot them up individually. Treat as any young plant.

quantity or those dealing with plants that are tricky to propagate) through medium-priced propagators to simple plastic bags (fine for the average gardener). The purpose of any type of apparatus is the same: to create a close, moist atmosphere around the cuttings so that they do not dry out.

Composts

A special compost (soil mix) called cutting compost is usually used. This will vary in composition, but is basically 50 per cent sand (for drainage) and 50 per cent a moisture-retaining medium (traditionally peat but now more likely to be a peat substitute).

Taking cuttings

Cuttings should be fresh growth that is not too soft and not too old. The shoot chosen should not have flower buds, or be in flower or seed. The best cuttings for most plants are basal ones – the young growth found at the base of a plant either in spring or after the plant has been cut to the ground later in the season. With a few plants, such as penstemons, you

can take cuttings from any part of a shoot, but normally you would just take them from the tip. Cuttings vary in length depending on the plant, but try to make them at least several pairs of leaves long – say, 3–7cm (1¼–3in) – or longer than this and then trim them off when potting them up. As soon as you have taken a cutting, put it in a plastic bag and seal it.

Striking cuttings

Now "strike" (pot up) your cuttings, as shown on the opposite page. Place cuttings in a hole made by a dibber or pencil, and firm the compost down, making sure that your cuttings' bottom leaves are above the level of the compost and that the leaves of different cuttings do not touch.

Aftercare

If your potted-on cuttings are in plastic bags, turn the bag inside out once a day to remove condensation. Keep the compost moist and make sure that the pot or propagator is in a light place, but out of the sun. Once roots have formed on the cuttings, pot them up in other pots.

Root cuttings

Some plants can be grown from a small piece of root. There aren't vast numbers of plants that suit this, but for some, such as pulsatilla or oriental poppies, it is the only effective reproductive method. The best time to take root cuttings is when a plant is dormant – usually winter. Because new growth often starts below ground well before the end of winter, the usual time for taking such cuttings is early winter.

Plants for root cuttings

Acanthus	Morisia
Anchusa	monanthos
Anemone x	Ostrowski
hybrida	magnifica
Campanula	Papaver orientale
Catananche	Phlox
Echcinops	Primula
Eryngium	denticulata
Gaillardia	Pulsatilla
Geranium	Romneya
Gypsophila	Stokesia laevis
Limonium	Symphytum
Macleaya	Trollius
Mertensia	Verbascum

Container gardening

All kinds of garden can benefit from the use of containers. In small patios or balconies, this may be the only form of gardening possible. In larger gardens, containers are used to add another dimension to the overall design – one of their great virtues is that they add a three-dimensional quality.

Types of container

A wide variety of containers are suitable for gardens and they are generally chosen for their visual suitability. The most crucial factor is that they must have a drainage hole, so that excess water can find its way out – waterlogged plants soon die.

Another issue is that they must be frost-proof if they are to stand outside in winter without the risk of cracking or shattering. Containers should also be secure. Those that are on windowsills or are hanging must obviously be very tightly attached so that they do not fall on anyone. Perhaps less obvious, but still very important, is that pots standing on the ground must be firmly planted so that they do not topple over if

knocked. A large pot filled with damp compost (soil mix) can be extremely heavy and could potentially cause a severe injury.

Which compost?

There are various composts on the market suitable for containers. Some are just called potting composts, while others claim to be specially formulated for containers. There is not much difference between them, and the final choice is personal and depends on what works best for you.

Some of the "container composts" differ from potting compost in that they contain special water-retaining granules. These hold an amazing amount of water and release it slowly for the plants' use without the compost becoming waterlogged. These granules are readily available to buy, in several forms, and can be added to any compost, so you are not restricted to composts that already contain them. The other thing that all composts contain is a slow-release fertilizer. This comes in the form of granules, which release their nutrients over a long period.

Getting the best results

As mentioned, all containers must have good drainage in the form of one or more holes at their lowest part. Cover these with broken bits of pot, tiles or irregularly shaped stones, so that water can pass out but the compost is retained.

If you are using plain compost, pour it straight from the bag into the container. If you want to add water-retaining granules, pour some compost into a bucket, mix in the granules at the suggested rate, and pour the mixture into the container.

PLANTING UP A CONTAINER

1 Cover the bottom of the container with small stones or some pieces of tile or pottery, so that water can drain freely from the pot.

2 Partly fill the pot with a good quality potting compost (soil mix). Loose slow-release fertilizer and water-retaining granules can also be mixed with the compost before the pot is filled.

3 Scoop a hole in the compost and insert the plant, positioning it so that the top of the root-ball (roots) will be level with the surface of the compost.

4 Place any extra plants you wish to include around the edge of the main plant. Add more compost to fill any gaps, and firm down.

5 Insert a fertilizer pellet if you have decided to use one, rather than the loose fertilizer granules. Water thoroughly.

PLANTING UP A HANGING BASKET

1 Stand the basket on a large pot or bucket, in order to make it easier to work with. Carefully place the basket liner in position so that it fills the basket. Half-fill the liner with compost, then mix in some water-retaining crystals, following the manufacturer's instructions, to help prevent the basket from drying out. Also add some slow-release fertilizer; this will remove the necessity to feed throughout the summer.

2 Cut holes about 4cm (1½in) across in the side of the liner. Shake some of the earth off the root-ball (roots) of one of the side plants and wrap it in a strip of plastic. Poke it through the hole, remove the plastic and spread the roots out. When all the side plants are in place, fill up your basket with compost, adding more water-retaining crystals and slow-release fertilizer.

3 Plant up the rest of the basket, packing the plants much more tightly together than you would in the open ground. Smooth out the surface of the compost, removing any excess or adding a little more as necessary. Water, then hang the basket indoors until all danger of frost has passed.

Firm down the compost and top up with more so that the surface is about 2–5cm (1–2in) below the container's rim (depending on its size).

A container full of compost can be very heavy, so place it in its final position before planting it up, or you may not be able to move it there. You could put it on a wheeled trolley sold especially for containers, ready to move into position.

Hanging baskets

Ever increasing in popularity, hanging baskets can provide a riot of colour all summer long. Most hanging baskets include tender annuals so they cannot be placed outside until after the last frosts, but they can be made up in advance and left indoors until the danger of frosts has passed, by which time the basket will have filled out and with luck be in full flower.

The most successful baskets are those in which the framework cannot be seen, as it is entirely masked by plants. In many cases, the hanging basket will look like a ball of plants.

Any combination of plants can be used to create different schemes. A wonderful pot-pourri of colours can be achieved with a mixed planting, although a more sophisticated effect can be created if you use plants in the same colour or even plants of just one variety.

Watering

Containers need watering every day, sometimes more in hot, sunny conditions. Water-retaining granules help to provide some moisture, but you will still have to water on most days when it doesn't rain. Smaller containers dry out quicker than large ones because of their higher ratio of surface area to volume.

Containers sheltered from the rain, and those that contain large plants whose leaves may prevent the rain reaching the compost, may need watering even after rain.

In winter it is important not to overwater; the compost should be just moist. Automatic watering systems can be installed if you have a lot of pots or if you are often away.

Feeding

Most composts use a slow-release fertilizer, which will often last long enough to see you through the season – check the manufacturer's instructions. If necessary, top-dress with more fertilizer, which is readily available. If you make your own garden compost, you can add a slow-release fertilizer either in granules or in the tablets, which are just pressed into the soil.

Popular annuals for hanging baskets

Anagallis	Lathyrus
Antirrhinum	Lurential
Asarina	Lobelia
Begonia	Myosotis
Bidens	Nicotiana
Brachycome	Pelargonium
Camissonia	Petunia
Cerinthe	Sanvitalia
Chrysanthemum	Schizanthus
Diascia	Senecio
Echium	Tagetes
Felicia	Tropaeolum
Fuchsia	Viola ×
Helichrysum	wittrockiana

Pests and diseases

Most gardeners fear pests and diseases more than anything else, and these fears are only exacerbated by the vast array of bottles, packets and sprays now found in garden centres and nurseries. In fact, serious garden problems are fairly rare and there is little reason for most gardeners to worry. The good news is that common sense is often preferable to a chemical armoury.

What causes trouble?

It is surprising how few pests and diseases actually affect perennials and annuals. Those pests that are a nuisance, such as slugs and rabbits, are big enough to be dealt with manually without recourse to chemicals. The other major pest is greenfly (aphids), but even they attack only a few plants and should not present a real threat.

Viral diseases can suddenly appear, with leaves and plants becoming distorted or discoloured, and you may need to resort to chemicals to halt their spread.

Mixed planting

Many of these problems can be overcome by having a mixed community of plants. Pests and diseases are less likely to catch hold in a mixed cottage garden than in one that specializes in just one type of plant. In the latter case, a disease is likely to affect all the plants, while in the former it will affect just a few plants, and therefore not become a serious threat. Any holes that are caused by losses from pest or disease damage will also not be so visible.

A mixed garden contains a large number of beneficial insects, which prey on the pest insects, and this results in a balanced community in which the pests will rarely get the upper hand.

Rabbits can cause a lot of damage to plants, as they have done here. Placing netting round the garden is the only solution.

Slugs and snails are two of the gardener's worst enemies. A night-time patrol with a torch will capture a lot of them at work.

Good hygiene

Another way of ensuring that diseases rarely get a hold is to practise good hygiene. Remove all dead and dying material from the beds and borders, and be alert for any signs of diseased material so that you can deal with the problem promptly. If viruses attack, remove and burn the affected plants.

Attacking the problem by hand

With the best will in the world, problems do occur. There can be few gardens, for example, where slugs are not a nuisance, especially in early spring when the succulent shoots are first appearing. You can, of course, try to use only "slug-proof" plants,

but when slugs are hungry they will eat most plants, so if you remove their favourite food, their tastes are likely to change. You can use slug bait if you are careful to ensure that pets and other animals cannot get at either the bait or the slugs once they have eaten it.

One of the best methods for getting rid of slugs is to go out in the evening as it gets dark with a torch and collect the emerging slugs in a bucket and dispose of them at some distance. (Don't throw them over your neighbour's fence: they will just crawl back and your neighbour will not be best pleased.) After a few nights, you will have reduced the population sufficiently

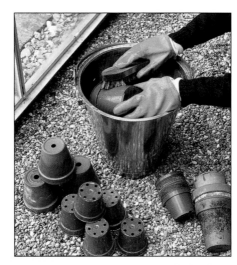

Cleaning pots by washing and scrubbing them is a good basic hygiene practice that will help prevent problems with young plants.

With some severe outbreaks of pests or diseases it may be necessary to resort, with great care, to the use of chemicals.

Damage by the caterpillars of moths and butterflies can ruin flowers. Picking them off by hand is the most effective treatment.

Greenfly and blackfly (aphids) are common pests. A mixed garden will usually provide sufficient predator insects to combat them.

Fungal diseases, such as this case of mildew, are a constant problem. Good hygiene and avoidance of overcrowding help.

so that they are no longer a problem, at least for a while. Caterpillars can also be removed by hand.

Rabbits are another big problem in some gardens. Here the only real solution is to place a rabbit-proof fence around the whole garden. You could just fence off individual borders, but the fencing does look ugly and is less obtrusive if placed around the whole boundary.

Small outbreaks of aphids can be left to other predators to deal with, but if they begin to accumulate you can remove them either by running your fingers up the stems and squashing them or by simply removing the stem.

Chemical means

There are chemicals available for dealing for most pests and diseases, and if your garden suffers a serious outbreak then you may need to resort to them. Do not, however, spray widely as a precautionary measure, and spray only the parts of the plant that are affected. It is very

important to follow the instructions on the bottle, packet or spray. At all costs avoid spraying the whole garden "just in case".

Regulations with regard to horticultural chemicals are in a state of flux and many traditional ones have been banned. Even some new ones leave the market only a few years after going on the shelves. Similarly, some chemicals are banned in some countries and not in others. So, if you need to treat a particular problem, consult your garden centre and make certain that you obtain something that is appropriate for your problem.

Natural predators

Introducing or encouraging beneficial insects can have a surprisingly dramatic impact on the number of pests in your garden. Check out which pests your plants are likely to fall prey to, and then simply encourage their natural predators into your garden.

Ladybirds (ladybugs) and larvae: eat aphids, scale insects, mealy bugs and caterpillars

Hoverflies and larvae: eat up to 50 aphids a day

Lacewings: eat aphids, woolly aphids, spider mites, scale insects and caterpillars

Ground beetles: eat slugs, flat worms, cabbage and carrot rootfly (eggs and larvae), vine weevils and spider mites

Anthocorid bugs: eat vine weevil larvae, caterpillars, midge larvae and spider mites

Centipedes: eat slugs and snails

Thorough soil preparation and good general hygiene routines will help to keep plants, such as this lovely wallflower, looking fresh and healthy.

Organic gardening

In recent years, organic gardening has moved to the forefront. Like so many other aspects of gardening, however, organic practice often involves little more than plain common sense: in this case, using only natural organic materials and not using inorganic (synthetically manufactured) substances unless absolutely essential. In other words, generally working with nature rather than against it. If you follow these rules in your garden, then you are pretty well organic already.

The chemicals issue

So, in essence, organic gardening amounts simply to gardening without the use of chemicals (although some naturally occurring chemicals are allowed).

Chemicals are often used by gardeners as a form of shortcut: it is so much easier to spray a border full of weeds than it is remove all of the weeds by hand. A slight change of

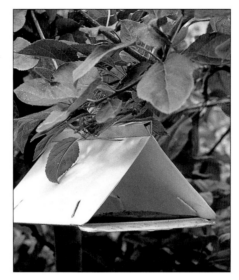
Sticky traps such as this use pheromones to attract insects, which then get trapped by the sticky substance inside.

mindset is all that is needed here. Gardeners need to try and accept that gardening is inherently a time-consuming occupation, and that it is far better to spend a bit more time on a chore rather than waste your money on all kinds of unnecessary chemicals.

Advantages of organic gardening

In terms of flower gardening specifically with annuals and perennials, the visual results of following organic principles are pretty minimal, but over time there are great advantages to the garden as a whole. If, for example, you treat the soil with well-rotted organic materials, such as garden compost (soil mix) or farmyard manure, then the structure of the soil will be improved and the plants fed at the same time. If, on the other hand, you just add chemical feeds to the soil, you will have well-grown plants, but, over the years, the structure of the soil will break down and in the long term plants will suffer.

A build-up of residues within the soil and run-off into watercourses is another problem that can develop if you use chemical fertilizers. They do not break down in the same way that organic fertilizers, such as bonemeal, do. The same is true of using

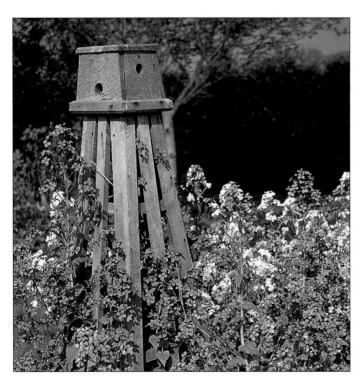
Try to provide places for lacewings and other beneficial insects to overwinter. This raised box, which has been stuffed with straw, is an ideal winter home for them.

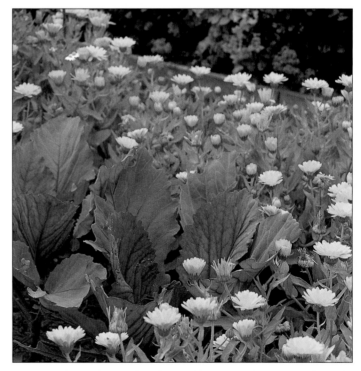
Pests may be confused and so deterred from attacking certain plants if the latter are surrounded by another very different type of plant, such as the marigolds seen here.

Surrounding prized plants with slug traps, such as this piece of guttering filled with water, may deter attacks.

chemicals to kill weeds or attack pests and diseases. Also, these chemicals often have unwanted side-effects. Pesticides aimed at killing greenfly (aphids) often also destroy beneficial insects such as bees, which are essential to gardening.

How can you be organic?

Starting with the soil, always try to use well-rotted organic material when preparing or top-dressing beds.

Friendly insects

Anthocorid bugs
Bees
Centipedes
Earwigs*
Ground beetles
Harvestmen
Lacewings
Ladybirds (ladybugs)
Parasitic wasps and flies
Rove beetles (commonly known as
   devil's coach and horses)
Spiders

*Often considered a nuisance because they eat the petals of some plants, such as dahlias. However, they also eat many pests.

You will find that this will improve the structure of the soil as well as providing nutrients.

If you need to feed plants, then choose organic fertilizers, such as bonemeal, made from naturally occurring materials. (Note that you will need to wear rubber/latex gloves when you are handling bonemeal preparations.) You can also make your own very effective foliar feeds for a quick pick-up by steeping nettles or comfrey in water and then watering or spraying the plants with the resulting liquid.

Always remove any weeds by hand, when you are digging over a bed, rather than resorting to chemicals. When you are preparing a new bed or border, rather than spray the whole thing with weedkiller, simply cover it with some black plastic sheeting or an old carpet – to deprive weeds of the light that they need to grow. When weeding existing borders, once again work by hand for the very best results.

Rid your borders of any slugs and caterpillars by manually removing them rather than killing them by bait, and keep a well-balanced border of mixed plantings, so that severe bouts of particular infestations are less likely to occur.

Encourage wildlife

Wildlife, such as birds and other animals, are fun to have in the garden. They are also beneficial. Although birds can be a nuisance in the fruit and vegetable garden (spreading some netting over vulnerable plants and trees should stop this), they are very useful in the flower garden as they eat a lot of pests, such as aphids and caterpillars.

Animals such as hedgehogs eat the worst enemy of most gardeners – the slug – while many garden birds make

The larvae of ladybirds eat incredible quantities of aphids and so are worth encouraging into the garden.

short work of snails. Flowers that attract ladybirds and lacewings are worth growing, as the larvae of these eat large quantities of greenfly.

Chemicals can be harmful to all these forms of wildlife, so this is another reason why they should be avoided if at all possible.

Birds love seed beds, so try to deter them by hanging shining kitchen foil above the bed to frighten them off.

Index

Collomia grandiflora

Anemone blanda and hellebores

Anemone ranunculoides

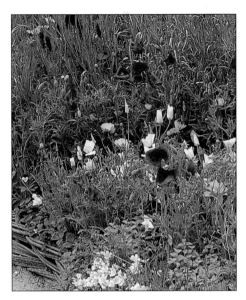

Limnanthes douglasii